Join us on the web at

EarlyChildEd.delmar.com

Group Time
Activities
A to Z

Joanne Matricardi
Jeanne McLarty

THOMSON
DELMAR LEARNING

Australia Canada Mexico Singapore Spain United Kingdom United States

THOMSON

★

TM

DELMAR LEARNING

Group Time Activities A to Z
Joanne Matricardi and Jeanne McLarty

Vice President, Career Education SBU:
Dawn Gerrain

Director of Editorial:
Sherry Gomoll

Acquisitions Editor:
Erin O'Connor

Editorial Assistant:
Stephanie Kelly

Director of Production:
Wendy A. Troeger

Production Manager:
JP Henkel

Production Editor:
Joy Kocsis

Production Assistant:
Angela Iula

Director of Marketing:
Wendy E. Mapstone

Channel Manager:
Kristin McNary

Marketing Coordinator:
David White

Cover Design:
Joseph Villanova

Composition:
Pre-Press Company, Inc.

Cover Image:
©Getty Images

Any additional questions about permissions can be submitted by email to thomsonrights@thomson.com

Library of Congress Cataloging-in-Publication Data

Matricardi, Joanne.
   Group time activities A to Z / Joanne Matricardi and Jeanne McLarty.
      p. cm. — (Activities A to Z series)
   Includes bibliographical references and index.
   ISBN 1-4018-7237-9
   1. Early childhood education—Activity programs.
I. McLarty, Jeanne.   II. Title.
   LB1139.35.A37M362 2005
   372.13—dc22

2005000022

NOTICE TO THE READER

Contents

Preface

Group time is an important aspect of the preschool curriculum. A kindergarten teacher was asked, "What should a child know before entering kindergarten?" She quickly replied, "How to sit still and follow directions." In the home, the preschooler may be the center of all activities. To be successful in school and in life, however, a child must learn how to participate as a member of a group.

As populations continue to swell, people wait in line wherever they go. Children need to learn patience and how to wait their turn in order to cope in our society. Patience, taking turns, following directions, and sitting still are all taught during an early childhood group time.

The purpose of *Group Time Activities A to Z* is to provide teachers, parents, and student teachers with a collection of group activities that promote social-emotional, physical, and cognitive development. Group participation involves more than just music and stories. Enrichment activities for math, social studies, language skills, and large motor activities are presented.

Many of the lessons presented include the use of patterns in creating materials. All suggested patterns are located in the appendix. The patterns are not meant for one-time use; materials should be carefully created and preserved for future service. The "Helpful Hints" section contains suggestions for material preservation.

The activities are presented in a lesson plan format. Sections included in each activity are "Developmental Goals," "Learning Objective," "Materials," "Adult Preparation," and "Procedures." The "Developmental Goals" offer social-emotional, physical, and cognitive concepts to be explored. The "Learning Objective" is a behavioral statement of the child's use of certain materials to accomplish the immediate goal of the lesson. The "Materials" section presents all supplies that are required, from preparation through implementation of the activity. The "Procedures" section lists the step-by-step process through which children in the group can successfully complete the lesson.

Additional sections may be included in the lesson plan. A "Notes" section may point out special considerations for the adult. "Variation," and "Expansion," sections are also sometimes included. A variation is an alternative suggestion for the activity—a means of changing the activity to accommodate a different theme. An expansion is a proposed means of enlarging the activity—by reading a book to the group, for example. (Always review a book before using it; some books may not be suitable for all children. If a book is too long, paraphrase the text to accommodate shorter attention spans.) "Book Suggestions" are given when reading is an integral component of the activity. "Safety Precautions" are presented when objects used may necessitate especially close supervision of children.

The activities in *Group Time Activities A to Z* are intended for use with the entire class. If activities would be more successful with a smaller group, this suggestion is given in the notes section. The size of the group will depend upon the children's needs and the adult/child ratio. A range of appropriate ages for each activity is given. This is just a suggestion; knowing the children's abilities and attention span will help determine what activities may be used and whether or not they need to be altered.

An "Index of Units" is provided to help select activities to accompany a theme-based curriculum. No matter how it is decided to implement these activities, remember: have fun! Enthusiasm is contagious.

HELPFUL HINTS

Through the years, we've developed strategies to make our group time activities proceed more smoothly. Some are helpful behavior management tools; others deal with the preservation of materials so that they may be used year after year. The following procedures have become routine in our classrooms.

BEHAVIOR MANAGEMENT TECHNIQUES

✂ The most important aspect of group time is that the adults enjoy the activity. Enthusiasm is contagious. Conversely, simply going through the motions of an activity will be noticed by the children, and their actions will reflect the adult's attitude.

✂ Be prepared. When the children come to group time, the adult should have the book, song, or other needed materials ready. Children will not sit still waiting for the activity to begin.

✂ Maintain eye contact with the children. This helps them to sit for longer periods and keeps them interested in the activity.

✂ When reading a book, hold the book open as it is read so children can see the pictures.

Know the material well enough to be able to comfortably glance away from the text. It is important to spend more time looking at the children than looking at the words.

✂ To maintain the children's interest in books, select books that reflect the child's level. Toddlers are comfortable with board books, which allow a hands-on experience without causing damage to the book. Two- and three-year-olds appreciate picture books, with large pictures and shorter text. Four- and five-year-olds will sit and listen to a story with fewer pictures and longer text, if it is read well.

✂ When selecting a book, make sure it is one that adults and children will enjoy. Books in which the voice can be varied for different characters always holds children's attention. Books with repetitive phrases that children can repeat provide wonderful language experiences.

✂ Always keep the group's age and attention span in mind when planning activities. Be flexible. An activity may need to be cut short if the group's attention is waning; a story may be paraphrased if it is too wordy for young children.

✂ When planning group time at the beginning of the school year, it is always best to plan for a shorter period; the time may be lengthened as the children's attention span matures. A general guide to begin the year would be as follows:

Age	Group Time Length
Two-year-olds	10 minutes
Three-year-olds	15 minutes
Four-year-olds	20 minutes
Five-year-olds	25 minutes

✂ Alternate quiet and active segments. Too many quiet plans many cause the children to lose interest. Too many active ones may cause them to become overstimulated.

✂ Young children may need designated sitting spaces. Each child's area may be defined by using the following:

- Chairs
- Sit-upons (such as laminated shapes, corresponding with the unit, that are labeled with each child's name)
- Carpet squares
- Masking tape (on the floor)
- Large rugs with areas (such as color blocks or letters of the alphabet) that can be assigned to individual children

✂ Use props with activities whenever possible, because this helps to keep the children's interest. Puppets also hold a very strong attraction for young children.

✂ Allow children to determine the extent of their participation in group time. Instead of forcing a reluctant child to participate, allow him or her to sit and observe. (It is best not to let nonparticipants engage in another activity, because that may pull other children's attention away from the group.) An observer may reap as many benefits from an activity as a participant. For example, the parents of a child who doesn't sing with the group sometimes report that the child constantly sings preschool songs at home.

✂ Divide the class into smaller groups when necessary. Make certain that all groups have interesting activities to engage them. If the adult needs to closely monitor one group, provide self-regulating activities for the other groups (e.g., puzzles, folder games, or books on tape).

SETTING THE ATMOSPHERE

✂ With each unit, use the children's art activities to decorate the room. This will reinforce the unit and encourage the children's self-esteem. Place their names where they are visible, making sure that you have one creation by each child so that feelings won't be hurt.

✂ Tape tissue paper over some of the fluorescent lights to create atmosphere. For example, use light blue for an ocean unit to give the room a blue tint, as though underwater.

✂ When taking imaginary trips with the group, use as many realistic features as possible (e.g., packing, snacking, resting). Display pictures of the area being visited to make the experience more authentic.

✂ Research the topics chosen for units. The local public library is a great resource. Some libraries even have story packs to accompany typical early childhood units. These story packs may include items in addition to easy-reading books, such as puppets or other props. A wealth of information is also available on the Internet.

PRESERVATION OF MATERIALS

✂ When creating materials, use rubber cement for gluing; white glue may cause paper to wrinkle.

✂ If possible, laminate all materials made with paper. If there isn't any access to a laminator, use clear, unpatterned contact paper to laminate materials. Another option is to check with the local school or office supply stores, which will laminate materials for a small fee. Heavy tag board may also be used to create durable patterns that can be used many times without being laminated.

✂ Store materials in resealable plastic bags. This allows the adult to see at a glance what is inside and makes storage in a filing cabinet or file box easier.

MISCELLANEOUS

✂ When placing laminated items on the floor, use masking tape to secure them in place. This will prevent the children from sliding when they stand on them.

✂ Making song posters encourages all adults in the room to sing along. Adult involvement is important in encouraging the children to participate. Adults should not feel self-conscious about the quality of their singing. Children are nonjudgmental and enjoy singing as a joyful experience.

✂ Song posters are also beneficial to preschoolers. Although these children cannot read, using a poster with the song written on it provides prereading enrichment by calling attention to the printed word. The use of illustrations on the poster can also help the children to identify the song.

✂ Some activities will work well for one group of children but not for others. This may vary from year to year. If an activity fails, do not assume that its failure was totally the adult's responsibility. The makeup of the group plays a large role in the success of an activity. Perhaps an activity that does not work well now may work better later in the year, when the children have matured. Always take time for reflection and self-evaluation after using an activity. Ask, "What made the activity a success?" or "Is there something that can be done to improve this experience next time?"

ANCILLARY MATERIAL

ONLINE COMPANION™

An Online Companion™ to *Group Time Activities A to Z* can be found at www.earlychilded.delmar.com. This resource contains additional group activities for young children. The activities are written in the same lesson plan format found in this book, including developmental goals, learning objectives, lists of materials, directions for adult preparation, and step-by-step procedures. The activities are easy to understand and implement, either in the preschool classroom or at home.

The *Group Time Activities A to Z Online Companion™* also provides links to related preschool sites. These links contain additional ideas, patterns, book sources, and other group time materials. The family letters that appear in Appendix B of this text are also available to download for classroom use.

ACKNOWLEDGMENTS

This book is an accumulation of original and shared ideas developed over 40 years of teaching young children. Many thanks to our co-workers, students, and their parents for sharing and experimenting with us.

We, and the editors at Thomson Delmar Learning, would also like to thank the following reviewers for their time, effort, and thoughtful contributions, which helped to shape the final text:

Patricia Capistron
Rocking Unicorn Preschool
West Chatham, MA

Meredith Chambers, M. Ed.
Truman College
Chicago, IL

Vicki Folds, Ed.D.
Broward Community College
Coconut Creek, FL

Judy Rose-Paterson
Childtime Children's Centers
Escondido, CA

Marilyn Rice, M.Ed.
Tuckaway Child Development
Richmond, VA

Brenda Schin
Child Care Consultant
Ballston Spa, NY

Joanne Matricardi
Jeanne McLarty

SUPPLIES NEEDED

Most early childhood programs operate on a limited budget. Many of the materials used in this book may be purchased at your local discount or dollar store. The shopping list that follows has been divided into seven categories: consumables, nonconsumables, equipment, clothing, kitchen equipment, food, and recyclable items. See Appendix B for three sample family letters that you can use when requesting specific items.

CONSUMABLE SUPPLIES

Alka-Seltzer®
Birthday candles
Black cups
Cellophane tape
Chalk
Clear contact paper
Construction paper
Copy paper
Cotton balls
Cotton swabs
Crayons
Crepe paper
Dish soap
Dry erase markers
Feathers
Felt
Foam shapes
Gloves (latex)
Gloves (plastic)
Glue
Hay
Hand lotion
Hook and loop tape
Hot glue sticks
Index cards
Markers (permanent)
Markers (water based)
Masking tape
Paper bags
  (lunch size)
Paper plates
Paper towels
Pencils

Pink lipstick
Pipe cleaners
Plastic straws
Poster board
Push pins
Recordable CD
Resealable plastic
  bags
Rickrack
Rubber bands
Rubber cement
Sponges
Staples
String
Sunscreen
Tag board
Tempera paint
Tissue paper
Valentine cards
Wax paper
Wrapping paper
  (solid colors)
Yarn

NON CONSUMABLE SUPPLIES

Art knife
Baskets
Beach bag
Blank audio tapes
Blanket
Blocks
Bucket
Cake candle holders

Calendar with
  detachable
  numbers
Candles
CD or tape of animal
  sounds
Cloth
Glow-in-the-dark
  star stickers
Hole punch
Large rectangular
  sponges
Pictures of farm
  animals
Pictures of sea
  creatures
Pictures of zoo
  animals
Pillowcase
Plastic apple
Plastic bucket
Plastic chips
Plastic eggs that can
  be opened and
  filled
Plastic fishbowl
Plastic headbands
Plastic pails and
  shovels
Plastic sheet
Rectangular rug
  (three feet long)
Scissors
Seashells
Sleeping bag

Small plastic animals
Smocks
Snap clothespins
Stapler
Stethoscope
Stuffed animals
Toothbrush
Toy police badge
Yardstick

EQUIPMENT

Balance beam
Camera
CD player
Chalkboard
Dry erase board
Flannel board
Hairbrush
Hot glue gun
Opaque projector
Parachute
Rhythm
  instruments
Round table
Small battery-
  operated lantern
Tape player/recorder
Toy cash
  register
Toy fire truck
Tray
Umbrella
  (child size)
Unbreakable mirror
Utility knife

CLOTHING

Hat
Garden hat
Mittens
Pants
Scarf
Shirt
Shoes
Socks (adult size)
Socks (child size)
Winter coat
Winter hat

KITCHEN EQUIPMENT

Big bowls
Clear plastic bowl
Cookie sheets

Hot air popcorn popper
Individual aluminum pans
Long-handled spoon
Measuring cups
Measuring spoons
Pitcher (child size)
Plastic bowls
Plastic spoons
Water bottles

FOOD

Apple
Butter
Cherry pie filling
Flour

Ground cinnamon
Liquid flavoring (from the spice aisle in the grocery store)
Peanuts in shell
Popcorn kernels
Pumpkin
Sugar
Tart shells
Vanilla
Yeast

RECYCLABLE ITEMS

15 ounce butter container with lid
3′ empty gift wrap tube

8–16 oz. milk carton
Addressed envelope with cancelled stamp
Egg cartons
Film canisters
Foam packing peanuts
Large appliance box
Large bag—3 ft.
Magazines
Milk bottle caps
Newspapers
Paint stir sticks
Paper grocery bags
Shredded paper

All About Me

AGES: 2¹/₂–5

DEVELOPMENTAL GOALS:

✂ To improve self-esteem

✂ To promote social development

LEARNING OBJECTIVE:

Using a lunch-size paper bag and items from home, the children will share special information about themselves with their classmates.

MATERIALS:

One lunch-size paper bag per child
Marker

ADULT PREPARATION:

1. Label a lunch-size paper bag with each child's name.
2. Prepare a letter to send home to the children's families, asking each family to help their child put items in the bag pertaining to him or her (a family picture, a favorite toy or book, and so on). Explain in the letter that the items need to be unbreakable, that they need to fit in the bag, and that they will be returned.
3. Attach a family letter to each child's bag.
4. On the designated day the bags are returned, place them in the group time area.

PROCEDURES:

1. Have the children sit in a circle around the bags.
2. Randomly select a bag.
3. Show the group the name on the bag. Ask, "Whose name is this?"

continued

All About Me continued

4. Invite the owner of the bag to stand and share the items in the bag with the group.

5. The child will show his or her items, one at a time, and pass them around the circle.

6. Repeat steps 2–5 until all children have had a turn.

Notes: If the group is large, limit the number of items that are placed in the bag. If a child forgets to bring in a bag, be prepared with that child's photo, a drawing he or she has done, or a favorite toy from the classroom.

EXPANSION:

Read *ABC, I Like Me!* by Nancy Carlson (New York: Penguin Group, 1997). This book contains large colorful illustrations of a pig who lists his positive traits in alphabetical order.

Animal Sounds

ADULT PREPARATION:

1. Find pictures of animals familiar to children.
2. Laminate pictures.
3. Record some animal sounds, or download animal sounds from the Internet (try Web sites such as <http://www.findsounds.com>).

PROCEDURES:

1. Have the children sit in a semicircle.
2. Hold up each card and ask children to identify the animal on it.
3. As animals are identified, place the cards on the floor where all children can see them.
4. When all animals have been identified, play the recording of animal sounds, pausing after each sound and selecting a child to choose the picture of the animal that makes the sound.
5. Repeat step 4 until the recording is finished.

EXPANSION:

Read *Cock-a-Moo-Moo* by Juliet Dallas-Conté (London: Macmillan Children's Books, 2001). Rooster forgets his crow and makes all the other animals' sounds, until a joyful resolution returns his cock-a-doodle-doo.

A

AGES: 1–5

DEVELOPMENTAL GOALS:

✂ To enhance the auditory senses

✂ To recognize familiar sounds

LEARNING OBJECTIVE:

Using pictures and tape-recorded sounds, the children will identify animals.

MATERIALS:

Tape recorder with blank tape, or CD player/burner with recordable CD
Pictures of animals
Laminating machine and film, or clear contact paper

Apple Hunt

AGES: 3–5

DEVELOPMENTAL GOALS:

✄ To promote name recognition

✄ To develop large and small muscle coordination

LEARNING OBJECTIVE:

Using paper apples and written names, the children will seek and find their names.

MATERIALS:

Apple pattern (Appendix A1)
Paper
Scissors
Marker
Bowl

ADULT PREPARATION:

1. Copy pattern and cut out two apples for each child.
2. Write each child's name on two apples.
3. Hide one set of the apples with names around the classroom.
4. Put the other set of apples in a bowl.

PROCEDURES:

1. Pass out the apples in the bowl to the children, giving each child the one bearing his or her name.
2. Tell children, "You are going on an apple hunt. What is written on your apple?"
3. Tell children that each of them needs to find the other apple with his or her name on it.
4. Send three to five children at a time to find their matching apples.

continued

Apple Hunt continued

EXPANSION:

Read *Johnny Appleseed* by Rosemary and Stephen Vincent Benét (New York: McElderry Books, 1961). The story of Johnny Appleseed is told in rhyme.

VARIATION:

With younger children, you may copy red, yellow, and green apples. Give each child one apple and have children find other apples that match their color.

AGES: 3–5

Apple, Apple, Who's Got the Apple?

DEVELOPMENTAL GOALS:

✄ To develop patience by taking turns

✄ To promote social development

LEARNING OBJECTIVE:

Using an apple and a chair, the children will participate in a game.

MATERIALS:

Apple (real or plastic)
Chair

ADULT PREPARATION:

1. Set a chair in front of the room, facing away from the group.
2. Place the apple under the chair.

PROCEDURES:

1. Have children sit on the floor in a semicircle.
2. Select one child to sit in the chair, facing away from the group.
3. Select another child to quietly take the apple and return to his or her seat.
4. Have the child who took the apple hide it behind his or her back.
5. The group then says, "Apple, apple, who's got the apple?"
6. The child in the chair turns around and gets three guesses as to who has the apple.
7. When a correct guess has been made, or after three guesses, the child in the chair exchanges seats with the child who has the apple.
8. The child holding the apple then places the apple under the chair and sits in the chair.
9. Steps 3–8 are repeated until everyone has a turn to take the apple and to sit in the chair.

EXPANSION:

Read *At the Orchard* by Elizabeth Sirimarco, photographs by David M. Budd. (San Juan Capistrano, CA: Child's World, 2000). Photographs accompany the simple text as apple production is shown from picking the fruit to being sold at the market.

Beach Bag Bingo

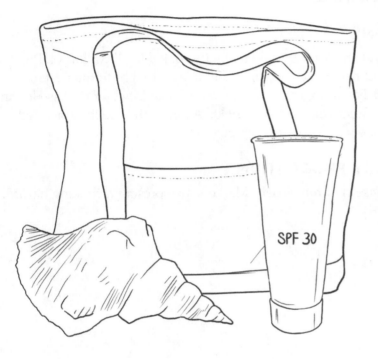

DEVELOPMENTAL GOALS:

✂ To improve visual discrimination

✂ To match objects that are the same

LEARNING OBJECTIVE:

Using a beach bag, bingo cards, and beach items, the children will play bingo.

MATERIALS:

Beach bag
Paper
Scissors
Beach bingo cards (Appendix A2)
Six markers (such as milk bottle caps or round plastic chips) for each child
Items found on bingo cards, such as a towel, beach ball, plastic bucket, hat, sunscreen, seashell, water bottle
Resealable plastic bag

ADULT PREPARATION:

1. Copy, enlarge, and cut out the bingo cards.
2. Cut the bingo cards using only six squares per child. Cut them in ways so not all of the cards are the same.
3. Put beach items in beach bag.

PROCEDURES:

1. Pass out bingo cards, giving one to each child.
2. Give each child six markers to place on the card.
3. Pull one item out of the beach bag and ask children to identify it.
4. Each child who has that item on his or her bingo card may cover that square with a marker.
5. Repeat steps 3–5 until all children have six markers on their bingo cards.
6. Ask children to help clean up by placing all the markers in the beach bag or a resealable plastic bag.
7. Store all items in the beach bag.

continued

Beach Bag Bingo continued

Note: Game may be played until the first child has placed all six markers on his or her card, with all children then clearing their cards to begin a new game.

EXPANSIONS:

Read *Bears at the Beach* by Niki Yektai (Brookfield, CT: Millbrook Press, 1996). Count bear beach activities and items brought to the beach, from 10–20. For younger children, read *A Beach Day* by Douglas Florian (New York: Greenwillow Books, 1990). A day at the beach is pictured, with only one to three words per picture.

⚠ SAFETY PRECAUTION:

Supervise children closely. Markers may present a choking hazard.

Beach Towels

ADULT PREPARATION:

1. Ask children to bring in a beach towel or large towel.
2. Have extra towels available for children who do not bring them.
3. Clear an area large enough to lay all the towels in a circle.

PROCEDURES:

1. Invite the children to sit on their towels.
2. Give each child a shovel and pail.
3. Tell the children that they are sitting on the beach and that they will play a game about following directions.
4. Ask the children to hold the pail *over* the towel.
5. Ask them to place the pail *on* the towel.
6. Ask them to put the shovel *in* the pail.
7. Ask them to place the pail *beside* the towel.
8. Ask them to turn the pail *over* and place the shovel *on top* of the pail.
9. Ask them to place the shovel *under* the pail.
10. Ask them to turn the pail *over* and pretend to fill it with sand.
11. Continue giving spatial directions as long as the activity holds the children's attention.

EXPANSION:

Read *Super Sand Castle Saturday* by Stuart J. Murphy (New York: HarperCollins, 1999). Sarah and Juan compete to build the tallest tower, deepest moat, and longest wall. They use the same type of objects to measure their activities, but their measurement tools are different sizes, giving them incorrect results until they both measure by the inch.

VARIATION:

Add seashells to the activity to increase the spatial directions given.

AGES: 3–5

DEVELOPMENTAL GOALS:

- ✂ To understand spatial relationships
- ✂ To follow directions

LEARNING OBJECTIVE:

Using beach towels, pails, and shovels, the children will follow spatial directions.

MATERIALS:

Beach towel (one for each child)
Plastic pail and shovel, or plastic bowl and spoon (one for each child)

9

Birthday Candles

AGES: 1–5

DEVELOPMENTAL GOALS:

✂ To improve self-esteem

✂ To promote social development

LEARNING OBJECTIVE:

Using candle holders, candles, and a butter container decorated as a cake, the children will recognize classmates' birthdays.

MATERIALS:

15-ounce butter container with lid
Scissors
Cake candle holders
Birthday candles
Felt
Rickrack
Glue

ADULT PREPARATION:

1. Glue felt around the bottom and sides of the butter container to resemble a cake.

2. Glue rickrack around the edges.

3. Cut small slits in the bottom of the butter container, as many slits as the age of the oldest child in your class plus one. This will allow for the number of candles needed to celebrate each child's birthday.

4. Glue candle holders in each slit.

5. Store with candles inside the butter container.

6. When a child is going to celebrate a birthday, place as many birthday candles as necessary in the holders.

PROCEDURES:

1. Have the birthday child come to the front of the group.

2. Place the birthday cake in front of the child.

3. Ask the group, "What are we celebrating today?"

continued

10

Birthday Candles continued

4. Ask, "How old is _____ today?"
5. Count the number of candles with the children.
6. Sing "Happy Birthday" with the group.
7. Invite the birthday child to pretend to blow out the candles.
8. Remove the candles one by one, counting backward. Or you may say, "If we take off this candle, how many candles are left?"

EXPANSIONS:

Have the birthday child remove the lid from the cake to find stickers inside. The child may select a sticker and then pass out the other stickers to the group. Or read *Benny Bakes a Cake* by Eve Rice (New York: Greenwillow Books, 1981). Benny helps bake his cake on his birthday, only to have his dog, Ralph, eat it. However, his dad and sister save the day.

AGES: 2–5

DEVELOPMENTAL GOALS:

✂ To improve dental health

✂ To expand vocabulary

LEARNING OBJECTIVE:

Using a song poster, the children will sing a song about brushing their teeth.

MATERIALS:

Poster board
Child brushing teeth pattern (Appendix A3)
Paper
Markers
Scissors
Rubber cement

Brush, Brush, Brush Your Teeth

ADULT PREPARATION:

1. Copy the pattern of the children brushing teeth.
2. Color, cut, and glue the pattern on poster board.
3. Using large print, write the words to the song, "Brush, Brush, Brush Your Teeth."
4. Hang the song poster where all can see it.

PROCEDURES:

1. The children and adults will sing the following song while pretending to brush their teeth.

Brush, Brush, Brush Your Teeth

(Sung to the tune of "Row, Row, Row Your Boat")

Brush, brush, brush your teeth.

Brush your cares away.

Up and down.

Up and down.

Plaque goes down the drain.

EXPANSION:

Read *Little Rabbit's Loose Tooth* by Lucy Bate (New York: Crown Publishers, 1975). Little Rabbit is anxious about losing her first tooth.

VARIATION:

Sing this song while children are brushing their teeth after meals or snacks.

Bunny Hop continued

6. Call all little bunnies to hop over to group time.

7. Have the bunnies stand in a circle and turn so they are ready to move clockwise.

8. Say, "Put your foot out."

9. Say, "Put your foot in."

10. Say, "Hop, hop, hop."

11. Say, "Put your other foot out."

12. Say, "Put your foot in."

13. Say, "Hop, hop, hop."

14. Say, "Wiggle your nose."

15. Say, "Scratch your ears."

16. Say, "Hop, hop, hop."

17. Ask the children, "What else do rabbits do?"

18. Use the children's suggestions to give additional directions for all the bunnies to follow.

19. Have them hop, hop, hop again.

EXPANSION:

Read *Hang On, Hopper!* by Marcus Pfister (New York: North-South Books, 1995). Hopper the rabbit tries to swim.

Bunny Hop

AGES: 4–5

DEVELOPMENT GOALS:

✂ To delight in movement

✂ To follow dir

LEARNING OBJECTIVE:

Using rabbit e
directions, the
will move by
like bunnies.

MATERIALS

White const
  paper
Rabbit ear p
  (Append
Copy pape
Stapler an
Scissors
Markers
Optional:
  cotton
  contai
  liquid
  dish s

ADULT PREPARATION:

1. Cut construction paper into 3" strips.
2. Staple strips in a circle to fit around each child's head, making one headband per child.
3. Write each child's name on a headband.
4. Copy the pattern of the rabbit ears, making two ears for each child.

PROCEDURES:

1. Have children color their rabbit ears.
2. Staple the ears to the sides of each child's headband.
3. Have children put on their bunny headbands.
4. Optional: Use a new tube of lipstick to make each child's nose pink. Lipstick may be applied with individual cotton swabs.
5. Optional: Mix brown liquid tempera paint with a squirt of dish soap and hand lotion. This may be applied with individual cotton swabs to the children's cheeks, to make whiskers.

continued

Bunny in a Basket

ADULT PREPARATION:

1. Place bunnies in a basket. The number of bunnies used will depend on the age and attention span of the children.

PROCEDURES:

1. The adult will count and show each bunny to the children.
2. Discuss the color and size (small, medium, large) of each bunny.
3. Tell the children to close or cover their eyes.
4. Holding the basket, the adult will turn their back to the children and remove one of the bunnies, hiding it from the children's view.
5. Place the basket where the group can see it.
6. Ask, "Which bunny is missing?"
7. Once the children have guessed correctly, repeat steps 3–6.

Note: If identifying one missing bunny is too easy for the children, try removing two bunnies at once.

EXPANSION:

Read *Are You Ready for Bed?* by Jane Johnson (New York: Scholastic, 2002). Mrs. Rabbit tries everything to get the youngest bunny to sleep. When she finally succeeds, guess who wakes up next?

DEVELOPMENTAL GOALS:

- ✄ To enhance memory skills
- ✄ To improve visual discrimination

LEARNING OBJECTIVE:

Using a basket and toy bunnies, the children will identify missing objects.

MATERIALS:

Basket
Two to six bunnies (stuffed or plastic)

B

Butterfly

DEVELOPMENTAL GOALS:

✂ To follow directions

✂ To promote role playing

LEARNING OBJECTIVE:

Using a book, sleeping bag, and tissue paper wings, the children will enact the metamorphosis from caterpillar to butterfly.

MATERIALS:

Sleeping bag
Tissue paper (several colors—full sheets)
Snap clothespin
Pipe cleaners
The Very Hungry Caterpillar by Eric Carle (New York: Philomel Books, 1969)

ADULT PREPARATION:

1. Lay a full-size sheet of tissue paper flat on a table, then lay two or three more sheets on top of it.
2. Fanfold the sheets.
3. Place the pipe cleaner around the middle of the folded sheets.
4. Twist the pipe cleaner to hold the tissue paper in place.
5. Open the fanfolds, spreading them to resemble butterfly wings.
6. Place the sleeping bag on the floor.
7. Unzip the bag halfway.
8. Hide the tissue paper wings inside the sleeping bag.

PROCEDURES:

1. Have children sit in a semicircle with the sleeping bag in front of the group.
2. The adult will sit behind the sleeping bag (on the zipper side), and read *The Very Hungry Caterpillar* to the group.

continued

Butterfly continued

3. Have one child act out the role of the caterpillar by pretending to eat and eat and eat and then lying down inside the sleeping bag.

4. When the child is in the bag, the adult will reach into the bag and fasten the wings on the child's back with a clothespin.

5. Zip the sleeping bag closed, keeping the child's face uncovered.

6. Ask the other children, "What happens next?"

7. Have the caterpillar child pretend to sleep and then to stretch and wake up.

8. Unzip the sleeping bag as the butterfly child emerges.

9. Repeat steps 3–8 until all children have been given an opportunity to be the caterpillar turning into a butterfly.

Note: The book may be read to your entire group, then break the class into smaller groups to act out the role of caterpillar and butterfly.

BOOK SUGGESTION:

The Very Hungry Caterpillar by Eric Carle (New York: Philomel Books, 1969). In this children's classic, a caterpillar eats through a large number of things, leaving holes in the book's pages. Finally, he spins a cocoon and turns into a beautiful butterfly.

B

AGES: 3–5

DEVELOPMENTAL GOALS:

✄ To recognize colors

✄ To enhance vocabulary

LEARNING OBJECTIVE:

Using a poster board, bee stick puppets, and flowers on sticks, the children will repeat a chant.

MATERIALS:

Bee pattern (Appendix A5)
Flower pattern (Appendix A6)
Paper
Scissors
Poster board
Markers
Rubber cement
Two baskets
Hot glue gun and glue sticks, or stapler and staples

Buzzing Bees

ADULT PREPARATION:

1. Copy the patterns of the bee and flower, making enough copies for the children to have one of each.
2. Color and cut out the bees and flowers, or have the children do this. The flowers need to be colored red, yellow, or purple.
3. Hot-glue or staple the bees to craft sticks, creating stick puppets.
4. Hot-glue or staple the flowers to craft sticks.
5. Copy, color, and cut out one additional bee and flower to glue on a poster board.
6. Using large print, write the words to the chant "Buzzing Bees" on the poster board.
7. Hang the poster at the children's eye level.

PROCEDURES:

1. Each child will hold a bee puppet in one hand and a stick flower in the other hand.
2. The child will repeat the words to the chant.
3. The bee puppets will move in the air until they are told to land on the color of flower held in the child's hand.
4. The bee puppet will then "sit on top" of the stick flower, until the bees are told to fly home.
5. The bees will fly to a basket on the floor. The children will put the bee puppets in the basket.
6. The children will place the flowers in the second basket.

Buzzing Bees

(The children hold a bee in one hand and a flower in the other hand.)

Adult: Bees are buzzing in the air.

Children: Bees are buzzing in the air. *(The children move their bee in the air.)*

Adult: In the air.

Children: In the air.

Adult: Looking for a flower.

Children: Looking for a flower.

Adult: Some bees will land on red flowers.

continued

Buzzing Bees continued

Children: Some bees will land on red flowers. (*The children holding red flowers will place their bee on their flower.*)

Adult: Some bees will land on yellow flowers.

Children: Some bees will land on yellow flowers. (*The children holding yellow flowers will place their bee on their flower.*)

Adult: Some bees will land on purple flowers.

Children: Some bees will land on purple flowers. (*The children holding purple flowers will place their bee on their flower.*)

Adult: All bees taste flower's nectar.

Children: All bees taste flower's nectar.

Adult: And fly back to their home.

Children: And fly back to their home. (*The children move their bee away from their flower in a flying motion.*)

EXPANSION:

Read *The Rose in My Garden* by Arnold Lobel (New York: Greenwillow Books, 1984). This story is told in the fashion of "The House That Jack Built." A bee is sleeping on a flower until a cat disturbs the chain of events.

C

AGES: 3–5

DEVELOPMENTAL GOALS:

✂ To recognize numbers

✂ To expand vocabulary

LEARNING OBJECTIVE:

Using the calendar and numbers, the children will recognize, identify, and count the numbers on the calendar.

MATERIALS:

Calendar
Detachable numbers
Hook and loop
   tape (to place on
   numbers and
   calendar)

Calendar

ADULT PREPARATION:

1. Purchase or create a calendar with detachable numbers. The calendar should be placed on the wall at the children's eye level or hung on a chart stand.

2. Place the appropriate month on the calendar.

3. Label the calendar with the days of the week, spelling out *Sunday*, *Monday*, and so on. (Do not use abbreviations.)

4. Place numbers on the calendar for each date that has already occurred in the current month, not including today's date (if it is May 3rd, only put the 1 and 2 on the calendar, so the children can add the 3).

PROCEDURES:

1. Ask the children, "What month is this?" If they do not give the correct response, tell them the name of the month.

2. Say, "Yesterday was [Tuesday]; what day is today?" If the response is incorrect, tell them the name of the day.

3. Tell the children, "Yesterday was the [10th]; what number is today?"

4. When the children have identified the number of today's date, count with them to that number, leading them in using a large muscle activity with each number counted (for instance, jump, clap, or stomp while counting).

5. Select a child to identify the number of the day among the detached numbers and put that number on the appropriate space on the calendar.

6. End by repeating with the children the day, month, date, and year ("Today is Thursday, December 11th, 2005").

EXPANSIONS:

Assign one child to be the weather person who looks out the window and chooses the appropriate weather symbol. (Suns, clouds, snowflakes, and raindrops may be purchased at school supply stores.) Fasten it to the appropriate date on the calendar. At the end of the month, count to see how many of each type of symbol is on the calendar. Make a monthly weather graph. Or read *Today Is Monday* by Eric Carle (New York: Scholastic, 1993). Using this book is a great way for children to learn the days of the week.

Clown Faces

AGES: 2–5

DEVELOPMENTAL GOALS:

✂ To promote role playing

✂ To understand rhythm

LEARNING OBJECTIVE:

Using music and movement, the children will make clown faces.

MATERIALS:

CD player and CD, or tape player and tape

ADULT PREPARATION:

1. Select music.

PROCEDURES:

1. Have children stand in a circle.

2. As the music plays, lead children in moving to the beat.

3. Stop the music at various points, and have the children make silly clown faces each time the music stops.

Note: Recordings are available with breaks in the music, eliminating the need to manually stop the music. For instance, try "The Freeze" on the CD or tape, *Kids in Motion*, by Greg & Steve (Youngheart Records, P. O. Box 27784, Los Angeles, CA 90027).

continued

Clown Faces continued

EXPANSIONS:

Children enjoy "reading" *Sing, Pierrot, Sing* by Tomie dePaola (San Diego: Harcourt Brace Jovanovich, 1983), a wordless picture book in which Pierrot tries to win the affection of a beautiful woman, unaware that her heart belongs to another. Pierrot is greatly saddened, until the friendship of children comforts him. For two-year-olds, read *Clowns* by Bob Reese (Provo, UT: ARO, 1995), a short, 10-word book showing a variety of clowns.

Color Hop

ADULT PREPARATION:

1. Trace or copy egg patterns and cut eggs out of construction paper, using construction paper that matches the colors of the plastic eggs.
2. Laminate the construction paper eggs.
3. Place the plastic eggs in a basket.
4. Using masking tape, tape the paper eggs in an open space on the floor where they are all visible.

PROCEDURES:

1. Hold up a plastic egg from the basket. Ask the children, "What color is this?" If the children do not respond correctly, tell them the correct answer.
2. Ask, "Where do you see a paper egg this color?"
3. When the matching paper egg has been found, repeat steps 1–2, identifying the color of each egg in the basket.
4. Ask the children to close their eyes.
5. Walk around the circle, carrying the basket, and ask each child to select an egg from the basket (with eyes still shut).
6. Have the children open their eyes and look at the eggs they selected.
7. Have each child hop to a paper egg matching his or her plastic egg.
8. When all children have matched their eggs, have them put their plastic eggs back into the basket.
9. Repeat steps 4–8.

EXPANSIONS:

Read *Colors* by Alvin Granowsky (Brookfield, CT: Copper Beech Books, 2001). Jo gets up and sees colors everywhere throughout her day (11 basic colors are the focus of this book). Or read *Planting a Rainbow* by Lois Ehlert (San Diego: Harcourt, 1988). Bright-colored illustrations show flowers in all the colors of the rainbow.

AGES: 2–5

DEVELOPMENTAL GOALS:

✂ To recognize colors
✂ To increase large muscle development

LEARNING OBJECTIVE:

Using paper eggs and plastic eggs, the children will match colors.

MATERIALS:

Egg pattern (Appendix A7)
Construction paper
Laminating machine and film, or clear contact paper
Scissors
Basket
Plastic eggs
Masking tape

Community Helpers

AGES: 2½–5

DEVELOPMENTAL GOALS:

✂ To identify community helpers

✂ To increase vocabulary

LEARNING OBJECTIVE:

Using pictures of community helpers, a bag, a stethoscope, a toothbrush, a badge, a fire truck, an envelope, and a small cash register, the children will match items to the occupation of those who use them.

MATERIALS:

Doctor pattern (Appendix A8)

Dentist pattern (Appendix A9)

Police officer pattern (Appendix A10)

Firefighter pattern (Appendix A11)

Mail carrier pattern (Appendix A12)

Store clerk pattern (Appendix A13)

Paper

Stethoscope

Toothbrush

continued

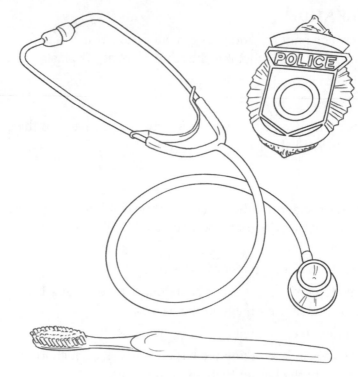

ADULT PREPARATION:

1. Copy the pictures of community helpers.
2. Laminate pictures.
3. Put the stethoscope, toothbrush, badge, fire truck, envelope, and cash register into the large bag or pillowcase.

PROCEDURES:

1. Hold up pictures of community helpers and ask the children to identify each one.
2. As the pictures are identified, place them on the floor in a row.
3. Pull one item out of the bag and pass it around the circle.
4. As the item is passed around, identify it and tell the children which type of community helper would use the item.
5. Ask the children how the item is used.

continued

Community Helpers continued

6. After all children have examined the item, have one child place it on the picture of the community helper who would use the item.

8. Repeat steps 3–6 with each item in the bag.

EXPANSION:

Read *Fire Fighter PiggyWiggy* by Christyan and Diane Fox (Brooklyn, NY: Handprint Books, 2001). This book contains large colorful pictures of what PiggyWiggy imagines it's like to be a firefighter.

Toy police badge
Toy fire truck
Addressed envelope
  with cancelled stamp
Small or toy cash
  register
Large bag or pillowcase

D

DEVELOPMENTAL GOALS:

- ✂ To match objects
- ✂ To recognize differences and similarities

LEARNING OBJECTIVE:

Using dinosaur cards, a dinosaur bingo board, and markers, the children will play bingo.

MATERIALS:

Dinosaur bingo cards (Appendix A14)
White paper
Laminating machine and film, or clear contact paper
Scissors
Rubber cement
Markers (such as milk bottle caps or round plastic chips)
Basket

Dinosaur Bingo

ADULT PREPARATION:

1. Copy, enlarge, color, laminate, and cut out various bingo cards. Make one for each child. Cut the bingo cards using only six squares per child. Cut them in ways so not all of the cards are the same.
2. Make additional bingo cards, one of each kind of dinosaur. Cut these dinosaurs apart and laminate them (these will be used as the draw cards).
3. Place the draw cards in a basket.

PROCEDURES:

1. Give each child a dinosaur bingo card and six marking chips.
2. Pull a dinosaur card out of the basket and ask the children to identify the dinosaur on it (help them, if necessary).
3. Tell the children to look for the same dinosaur on their bingo boards. Each child who finds a matching dinosaur on his or her bingo board may put a marker on that dinosaur.
4. Repeat steps 2–3 until all of the children's dinosaurs are covered with markers.

EXPANSION:

Read *If the Dinosaurs Came Back* by Bernard Most (San Diego: Harcourt, Inc., 1978). The author imagines all they ways dinosaurs would be useful to people if they were alive today.

⛔ SAFETY PRECAUTION:

Do not use markers that are smaller than a choke tube with children under the age of 3.

Dinosaur Stomp

Ages: 2½–5

DEVELOPMENTAL GOALS:

- ✂ To increase large muscle skills
- ✂ To improve listening skills

LEARNING OBJECTIVE:

Using a book, dinosaur hats, and dinosaur scales, the children will move like dinosaurs and listen to a story.

MATERIALS:

Paper plates
Scissors
Stapler and staples
Hole punch
Yarn
Construction paper
Crayons
Dinosaur book

ADULT PREPARATION:

1. To make dinosaur hats, cut the centers out of paper plates (one for each child).
2. Punch two holes in opposite edges of each plate.
3. Tie a 12" piece of yarn through each hole.
4. Cut construction paper into 4" wide pieces with zigzag edges.
5. Staple the zigzag pieces together to make 2' lengths.
6. Staple these "dinosaur scales" to the back of each hat.
7. Select a dinosaur book to read; suggestions are listed.

PROCEDURES:

1. Have the children color their dinosaur hats and scales.
2. Have the children put on their hats and tie them under their chins (some may need assistance).
3. Begin giving directions for the children to follow by saying, "Let's stomp to group time."
4. Say, "Move quietly to the door."

continued

Dinosaur Stomp continued

5. Say, "Stomp to the table."

6. Say, "Swing your tail to group time."

7. Say, "Sit down, but be careful not to sit on your tail!"

8. Continue giving directions as long as the children's attention span allows, then have the children sit in their designated group area.

9. Children will listen to a dinosaur story.

BOOK SUGGESTIONS:

Count-a-saurus by Nancy Blumehthal (New York: Scholastic, Inc., 1989). Different types of dinosaurs are counted up to ten. Pronunciations are given for the dinosaur names.

Danny and the Dinosaur by Syd Hoff. (New York: HarperCollins, 1958). Danny rides a dinosaur out of the museum and plays with him all day.

Drop the Apple

ADULT PREPARATION:

1. Cut an apple shape from a sponge.

PROCEDURES:

1. Have the children sit in a circle on the floor.
2. The adult will walk around the outside of the circle and quietly set the apple behind one child.
3. Continue to walk around the circle.
4. When the child notices the apple behind his or her back, that child will pick up the apple and chase after the adult.
5. The adult will then sit in the child's vacated spot.
6. The child then will walk around the outside of the circle and quietly set the apple down behind another child.
7. Continue the game until all children have had a turn.

EXPANSION:

Read *Apples* by Gail Gibbons (New York: Holiday House, 2000). *Apples* explores the history and process of apple production, with detailed sections on planting and caring for apple trees. It also includes illustrations of different varieties of apples.

Ages: 2¹⁄₂–5

DEVELOPMENTAL GOALS:

- ✂ To promote social development
- ✂ To develop patience by taking turns

LEARNING OBJECTIVE:

Using a sponge apple, the children will participate in a game.

MATERIALS:

Sponge
Scissors or art knife

Egg Hunt

DEVELOPMENTAL GOALS:

✂ To improve counting skills

✂ To understand one-to-one correspondence

LEARNING OBJECTIVE:

Using egg cartons and plastic eggs, the children will work in pairs to find and count twelve eggs.

MATERIALS:

Dozen-size egg cartons (one for each pair of children)
Construction paper
Stapler and staples
Plastic eggs (six per child)

ADULT PREPARATION:

1. Cut construction paper into 18" × 4" strips.
2. Fold each strip twice, so that the folded strips are 18" by 1" in size.
3. Cut the lids off egg cartons.
4. Staple one end of each folded strip to one end of an egg carton, then the other end of that strip to the other end of that carton, making a handle for the "basket."
5. Place plastic eggs throughout the room.

PROCEDURES:

1. At group time, the adult will divide the children into pairs.
2. Give each pair an egg carton with a handle attached.
3. As a group, count each cup in one carton, counting to 12.
4. Have each pair of children find and count 12 eggs, putting one egg into each cup of their carton.
5. When the cartons are full, have the children return to the designated group area.
6. When all the children have returned to the group, have the group count their eggs together.

Egg-cellent Sounds

ADULT PREPARATION:

1. Place one plastic animal in each egg.
2. Put eggs in the basket.

PROCEDURES:

1. Have one child select an egg from the basket, open the egg, and hold up the animal found inside.
2. Ask the child to identify the animal.
3. Ask the child to make the sound that animal makes.
4. Ask all of the children to repeat the sound.
5. Repeat steps 1–4 until all of the children have had a turn to select an egg and make the sound of the animal inside it.

Note: Try to use animals that hatch from eggs for this activity. If using animals that do not come from eggs, explain to the children which animals do not hatch from eggs.

EXPANSION:

Read *Seven Eggs* by Meredith Hooper (New York: Harper & Row, 1985). This is a wonderful, simple book that shows some animals that hatch from eggs.

AGES: 2–5

DEVELOPMENTAL GOALS:

✂ To demonstrate animal sounds
✂ To improve fine motor skills

LEARNING OBJECTIVE:

Using plastic eggs and plastic animals, the children will imitate animal sounds.

MATERIALS:

Plastic eggs
Small plastic animals that will fit into eggs
Basket

E

AGES: 2–5

DEVELOPMENTAL GOALS:

- ✂ To develop muscles
- ✂ To expand vocabulary

LEARNING OBJECTIVE:

Using a song and body motions, the children will sing and move like elephants do.

MATERIALS:

None needed

Elephants

ADULT PREPARATION:

1. Become familiar with the song "The Elephant."

PROCEDURES:

1. Lead children in bending at the waist with hands clasped and arms hanging low. (The clasped hands and arms simulate an elephant's trunk.)

2. Lead children as they move in a circle with slow, lumbering motions, singing the following song:

The Elephant

(sung to the tune of "Twinkle, Twinkle, Little Star")

The elephant comes from afar.

He is bigger than a car.

He likes to walk with all his friends.

They walk until they reach the end! [*Children stop abruptly and turn.*]

The elephant comes from afar.

He is bigger than a car.

continued

Elephants continued

EXPANSION:

Read "*Stand Back," Said the Elephant, "I'm Going to Sneeze!*" by Patricia Thomas (New York: Lothrop, Lee, & Shepard, 1971). Find out why all the animals did not want the elephant to sneeze and what happened when he didn't sneeze.

Farmer in the Dell

AGES: 3–5

DEVELOPMENTAL GOALS:

✄ To acquire social skills

✄ To increase large muscle development

LEARNING OBJECTIVE:

Using the song "The Farmer in the Dell," the children will act out the words of a song.

MATERIALS:

None needed

ADULT PREPARATION:

1. Clear a large area so the children can move in a circle.

PROCEDURES:

1. Have everyone in the group hold hands as they move in a circle and sing, "The farmer in the dell, the farmer in the dell, heigh-ho, the derry-o, the farmer in the dell."

2. Choose one child to be the farmer and have that child stand in the center of the circle as the group continues to hold hands and circle around, singing, "The farmer takes a wife, the farmer takes a wife, heigh-ho, the derry-o, the farmer takes a wife."

3. The farmer picks one child to be the wife. The wife joins the farmer in the circle as the group continues to hold hands and circle around, singing, "The wife takes a child, the wife takes a child, heigh-ho, the derry-o, the wife takes a child."

4. The wife picks one child to be the child. The child joins the others in the circle as the group continues to hold hands and circle around, singing, "The child takes a dog, the child takes a dog, heigh-ho, the derry-o, the child takes a dog."

5. The child picks one child to be the dog. The dog joins the others in the circle as the group continues to hold hands and circle around, singing, "The dog takes a cat, the dog takes a cat, heigh-ho, the derry-o, the dog takes a cat."

6. The dog picks one child to be the cat. The cat joins the others in the circle as the group continues to hold hands and circle around, singing, "The cat takes a rat, the cat takes a rat, heigh-ho, the derry-o, the cat takes a rat."

7. The cat picks one child to be the rat. The rat joins the others in the circle as the group continues to hold hands and circle around, singing, "The rat takes the cheese, the rat takes the cheese, heigh-ho, the derry-o, the rat takes the cheese."

8. The rat picks one child to be the cheese. The cheese joins the others in the circle as the group continues to hold hands and circle around, singing, "The cheese stands alone, the cheese stands alone, heigh-ho, the derry-o, the cheese stands alone."

continued

Farmer in the Dell continued

9. The cheese remains in the middle of the circle as all the others in the center rejoin the circle.

10. Repeat steps 1–9 until all children have a turn to be in the center of the circle.

EXPANSION:

Read *The Farmer in the Dell*, illustrated by John O'Brien (Honesdale, PA: Boyds Mills Press, 2000). Take a look at O'Brien's humorous twist on this traditional tale.

F

Feed the Elephant

DEVELOPMENTAL GOALS:

✂ To develop eye-hand coordination

✂ To develop social skills by taking turns

LEARNING OBJECTIVE:

Using a gift-wrap tube and peanuts, the children will pretend to feed an elephant.

MATERIALS:

3' empty gift-wrap tube
Masking tape
Construction paper
Markers
Scissors
Peanuts in the shell
   (use foam packing
   peanuts if any
   children are
   allergic to nuts)
Large bowl
Yarn
Hole punch
Round table
Newspaper

ADULT PREPARATION:

1. Punch a hole in one end of the empty gift-wrap tube.

2. Tie a 3' length of yarn to the hole punched at the end of the tube.

3. Turn a round table onto its side and tape the other end of the tube to the center of the table. (This tube will be the trunk of the elephant.)

4. Cut large ovals (for eyes) out of construction paper.

5. Using a marker, color the pupils of the eyes.

6. Tape the eyes on the table above the trunk.

7. Place newspaper on the floor under the trunk.

8. Place peanuts in a bowl on the floor under the trunk.

PROCEDURES:

1. The adult will hold the end of the yarn and stand behind the table to raise and lower the trunk by pulling the yarn.

2. Pull the yarn to hold the trunk in a slightly inclined position.

3. Have the children take turns feeding the elephant by placing peanuts in the trunk.

continued

Feed the Elephant continued

4. When the elephant is "full," raise the trunk and then lower it so all the peanuts will spill back into the bowl.

5. Repeat steps 2–4.

EXPANSIONS:

✄ Allow each child to count a set number of peanuts while feeding the elephant, or have the group count the total number of peanuts the elephant eats before getting full.

✄ Read *George* by Paul Borovsky (New York: Greenwillow Books, 1990). George the dog learns how to talk and teaches the animals in the zoo how to talk. Soon all the animals are talking to the zookeeper: the elephant complains about eating grass again, and the other animals have something to say, too.

⚠ SAFETY PRECAUTION:

Supervise children closely, because peanuts may present a choking hazard.

Fishbowl Rhymes

AGES: 4–5

DEVELOPMENTAL GOALS:

✂ To increase verbal skills

✂ To enhance vocabulary

LEARNING OBJECTIVE:

Using a plastic fishbowl, paper fish, and pictures, the children will match rhyming words.

MATERIALS:

Plastic fishbowl or clear plastic bowl

Red and blue construction paper

Fish pattern (Appendix A15)

Rubber cement

Scissors

Magazine pictures

ADULT PREPARATION:

1. Trace the fish pattern and cut blue and red fish out of construction paper.
2. Find pictures of pairs of objects that rhyme (such as pictures of a man and a pan or a fan, the moon and a spoon, a tie and a pie, a rug and a bug) in magazines, and cut them out.
3. Using rubber cement, glue one picture from each pair on a blue fish.
4. Glue the rhyming mates on the red fish.
5. When the glue dries, place the red fish in the plastic fishbowl.
6. Lay the blue fish face down in a row on the floor.

PROCEDURES:

1. The children will each turn over a blue fish and identify the picture on it.
2. When all the blue fish have been turned over, the children will each select a red fish from the bowl and identify the picture on it.

continued

Fishbowl Rhymes continued

3. The children will each find a blue fish whose picture rhymes with that of the red fish drawn from the bowl.

4. If a child has difficulty finding the rhyming picture on a blue fish for his or her red fish, the group may give assistance.

EXPANSION:

Read *Swimmy* by Leo Lionni (New York: Scholastic, 1963). This Caldecott Honor book shows Swimmy's adventures in the sea. It's a great help in beginning a discussion of all the different animals that live in the sea and how they work together.

VARIATION:

Place all of the fish in the bowl. When each child selects a fish from the bowl, have him or her name something that rhymes with the picture on that fish. This is a higher-level skill; the skill of matching rhyming pictured objects (as demonstrated in the foregoing activity) must be mastered first.

Five Frogs Are We

AGES: 2½–5

DEVELOPMENTAL GOALS:

- ✂ To recognize numbers
- ✂ To practice counting

LEARNING OBJECTIVE:

Using frog stick puppets, the children will sing a song.

MATERIALS:

Frog pattern (Appendix A16)
Poster board or tag board
Five paint stir sticks
Markers
Stapler and staples

ADULT PREPARATION:

1. Copy frog pattern five times on poster board or tag board.
2. Color and cut out the frogs.
3. Write the numbers 1–5 on the frogs.
4. Staple the frogs to the paint stir sticks, creating stick puppets.

PROCEDURES:

1. Select five children to hold the frog puppets and have them stand in front of the group in a line.
2. As the group sings the following song, the first child in the line of children holding frog puppets will jump and then sit down on the floor, until all five "frogs" are seated.

Five Frogs Are We

(sung to the tune of "I'm a Little Teapot")

Five frogs are we,

Clinging to a tree.

We are as happy as can be.

A fly comes along that we can see.

One of us jumps, and now there are four!

Four frogs are we,

Clinging to a tree.

We are as happy as can be.

A fly comes along that we can see.

One of us jumps, and now there are three!

Three frogs are we,

Clinging to a tree.

We are as happy as can be.

A fly comes along that we can see.

One of us jumps, and now there are two!

Two frogs are we,

Clinging to a tree.

We are as happy as can be.

A fly comes along that we can see.

continued

Five Frogs Are We continued

One of us jumps, and now there is one!

One frog is left,

Clinging to the tree.

It is as happy as can be.

A fly comes along that it can see.

It jumps off, and now there is none!

EXPANSIONS:

✂ Read *An Extraordinary Egg* by Leo Lionni (New York: Knopf, 1994). A frog finds a stone and brings it to her friends, who pronounce it a chicken egg. None of them realize what type of egg it really is until an alligator hatches from it!

✂ Read *Finklehopper Frog* by Irene Livingston (Berkeley, CA: Tricycle Press, 2003). Finklehopper Frog gets a new jogging suit before joining the other animals as they jog. Much to his dismay, they laugh at his suit and at the way he jumps instead of jogs. He feels terrible, until Rabbit comes along and helps him accept himself for who he is.

Flowers Start as Tiny Little Seeds

AGES: 2–5

DEVELOPMENTAL GOALS:

✂ To coordinate muscle development

✂ To understand how to follow directions

LEARNING OBJECTIVE:

By following directions, the children will act out a chant.

MATERIALS:

Poster board
Flower pattern (Appendix A6)
Copy paper
Rubber cement
Scissors
Markers

ADULT PREPARATION:

1. Copy, color, and cut out two or more flower patterns.
2. Glue the flowers on the poster board.
3. Write the words to "Flowers Start as Tiny Little Seeds" on the poster board and place it where you can see it while leading the chant.

PROCEDURES:

1. Say the chant and model the actions for the children.
2. Have children act out the actions in the song as you say it again.
3. As children become familiar with the chant, have them join you in saying the words.

   Flowers Start as Tiny Little Seeds

   Flowers start as tiny little seeds [*children ball themselves up on the floor*]

   Balled up in the earth,

   Balled up in the earth,

continued

Flowers Start as Tiny Little Seeds continued

Where none can see.

With rain and sun they start to grow. *[fingers make raining motion, then arms make a circle, for the sun]*

They poke through the earth, *[children begin to stand]*

And begin to show.

They stand up high, *[children are standing]*

Reaching for the sun. *[children's arms reach up high]*

Bending in the wind *[children bend and sway]*

Can be such fun.

Flowers start as tiny little seeds *[children return to balled-up positions on the floor]*

Balled up in the earth,

Where none can see.

EXPANSION:

Read *The Tiny Seed* by Eric Carle (New York: Simon & Schuster, 1987). The journey of a tiny seed is followed throughout a year, until it becomes the largest flower anyone has ever seen.

Garden Toss

AGES: 2–5

DEVELOPMENTAL GOALS:

✂ To understand the concept of gardening

✂ To promote role playing

LEARNING OBJECTIVE:

Using a gardening cube, the child will role-play different gardening techniques.

MATERIALS:

8- to 16-ounce milk carton

Copy paper

Scissors

Glue

Watering can pattern (Appendix A17)

Shovel pattern (Appendix A18)

Garden gloves pattern (Appendix A19)

Spade pattern (Appendix A20)

Seeds pattern (Appendix A21)

Small flower pattern (Appendix A22)

ADULT PREPARATION:

1. Make a gardening cube by taking an individual milk carton and stapling the peaked end flat.

2. Copy the gardening patterns.

3. Cut the pictures apart and glue one on each side of the cube.

PROCEDURES:

1. Show children the pictures on the cube.

2. Discuss how each pictured object is used in gardening.

3. Have the children take turns tossing the cube and identifying the picture that is facing up.

4. As each picture is identified, have children pretend to perform the action required to use that gardening object.

EXPANSION:

Read *This Year's Garden* by Cynthia Rylant (New York: Bradbury Press, 1984), which discusses a family's adventures in planting a garden.

Gather the Leaves

ADULT PREPARATION:

1. Ask children to bring in a variety of leaves. (You may need to provide some, also, to be sure that you have enough of different colors and shapes.)
2. Place leaves in a basket.
3. Lay paper plates on the floor in a line.

PROCEDURES:

1. Have children sit in a semicircle.
2. Ask the first child to select a leaf from the basket and put it on the first paper plate.
3. Ask the group, "What color is the leaf?"
4. Ask the children to describe the leaf's shape (pointy, round, etc.; you may need to help with this).
5. Have the second child select a leaf from the basket.
6. Ask the children, "What color is the leaf?"
7. Ask the children, "Is it the same shape as the first leaf?"
8. Tell the child who selected the leaf, "If the leaf is different from [first child]'s leaf, you may put it on the next plate. If the leaf is the same as [first child]'s leaf, you may put it with [first child]'s leaf."
9. Continue with all children taking turns selecting and sorting leaves.

EXPANSIONS:

✄ When all leaves are sorted, ask the children to count the number of each kind of leaf. The adult may write those numbers on the plates where the leaves lie. Children may then arrange the leaves and plates from the least number to the highest number.

✄ Read *Autumn Leaves* by Ken Robbins (New York: Scholastic Press, 1998), which features 13 different trees and their distinct leaves, using simple text and colorful photographs.

VARIATION:

Write numbers on paper plates. Children identify numbers, count, and place that many leaves on each plate.

AGES: 4–5; can use with ages 2–3 by just matching colors instead of colors and shapes

DEVELOPMENTAL GOALS:

✄ To identify colors

✄ To discriminate between objects that are the same and those that are different

LEARNING OBJECTIVE:

Using leaves, the children will match colors and shapes.

MATERIALS:

Leaves
Basket
Paper plates

Go Fly a Kite

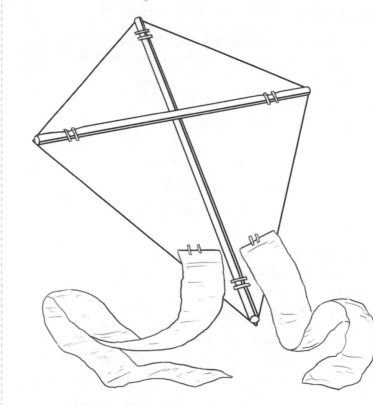

AGES: 2–5

DEVELOPMENTAL GOALS:

- ✂ To delight in rhythm and motion
- ✂ To increase vocabulary

LEARNING OBJECTIVE:

Using a construction paper kite and a song, the children will move their kites and their bodies in time with the music.

MATERIALS:

Construction paper
Scissors
Plastic straws
Stapler and staples
Crepe paper streamers

ADULT PREPARATION:

1. Cut construction paper into a diamond shape the length of the plastic straw.
2. Staple plastic straws on the back of the diamond in a T formation. If any part of a straw protrudes past the edge of the construction paper, trim it with scissors. Attach crepe paper streamers as the kite's tail.

PROCEDURES:

1. Have children hold their kites by the straws.
2. Ask children to move their kites while singing the following song:

Go, Go Fly a Kite

(sung to the tune of "Row, Row, Row Your Boat")

Go, go fly a kite

High in the air.

Swooping, spinning, skipping, swirling,

The wind takes it everywhere.

continued

Go Fly a Kite continued

Note: After step 1 of Adult Preparation, children may color their own diamonds with markers or crayons.

EXPANSION:

Read *Curious George Flies a Kite* by Margret Rey (Boston: Houghton Mifflin, 1958). George gets into trouble, as usual. Begin reading at the part of the story dealing with the kite (a little over halfway through the book) for children with shorter attention spans.

 ## SAFETY PRECAUTION:

The length of the streamers must not exceed 12 inches. This is to prevent accidental injury.

Hayride

AGES: 2–5

DEVELOPMENTAL GOALS:

✂ To improve auditory discrimination

✂ To acquire social skills

LEARNING OBJECTIVE:

Using a large box, hay, farm scenes, pictures of farm animals, and recorded farm animal sounds, the children will pretend to go on a hayride.

MATERIALS:

Large appliance box
Hay or shredded paper
Pictures of farm scenes
Pictures of farm animals
CD or tape of farm animal sounds
CD or tape player

ADULT PREPARATION:

1. Place hay in a large box. (If any children are allergic to hay, use shredded paper.)
2. Put up pictures of farm animals and farm scenes around the room.
3. Set up the CD or tape player with farm animal sounds.

PROCEDURES:

1. Divide the class into smaller groups, depending on the size of the box. (Each group should be small enough for all children to sit in the box.)
2. Invite children to climb aboard the "hay wagon."
3. Explain to children that some hay wagons are pulled by a tractor or horses.
4. Have the children pretend that they are bumping along on the farm while you play the recorded animal sounds.
5. Point to pictures matching the sounds as they play. (Be prepared to offer more explanations if needed.)

EXPANSIONS:

✂ Sing "Old MacDonald Had a Farm."

✂ Read *Duck on a Bike* by David Shannon (New York: Scholastic, 2002). This book has large, colorful pictures showing a duck riding a bike all over the farm. The other animals wonder why the duck would want to ride a bike, but soon they find out the answer when all of them have bikes to ride. The animals sounds are included, which delights younger children.

Hide the Gift

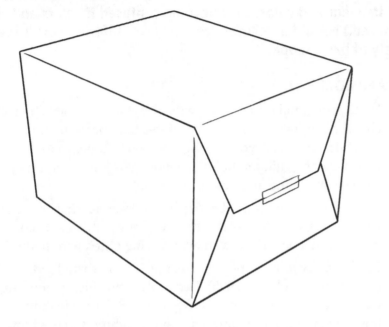

ADULT PREPARATION:

1. Wrap empty boxes as though they are gifts (one per child).
2. Cut construction paper squares to match the colors of the gifts (one for each color used).
3. Laminate the squares.
4. Tape the squares an equal distance apart, in the group time area.

PROCEDURES:

1. Have the children search the room for presents, asking them to each find one present.
2. As each child finds a present, ask him or her to tell you the color of the gift.
3. After a child has identified the color of the gift found, ask the child to stand on or near the square matching that color.
4. Once all children have found the matching squares for their gifts, ask them to hide the presents.
5. Have the children return to the group area.
6. Repeat steps 1–3.

continued

H

AGES: 3–5

DEVELOPMENTAL GOALS:

✂ To identify colors

✂ To match colors

LEARNING OBJECTIVE:

Using paper squares and gifts wrapped in solid-color paper, the children will match and sort colors.

MATERIALS:

Empty boxes—one for each child
Solid colored wrapping paper or tissue paper
Cellophane tape
Scissors
Construction paper to match gift paper
Laminating machine and film, or clear contact paper
Masking tape

Hide the Gift continued

Note: The construction paper may be cut into other shapes besides squares. For younger children, make all of the colors the same shape. (Children learning colors may become confused if colors and shapes are mixed.) For older children, you may cut different colors into a variety of basic shapes.

EXPANSIONS:

✄ Write sequential numbers on gifts of the same color. When all children are standing near the squares that match their gifts, have the children in each color group line up in numerical order (e.g., have the children holding yellow gifts and standing by the yellow square line up in order from 1–5).

✄ Read *Gifts* by Phyllis Limbacher Tildes (Watertown, MA: Charlesbridge, 1997). As this story explains, not all gifts come wrapped in a box. Here, a small girl is delighted with nature's gifts.

✄ Read *Gifts* by Jo Ellen Bogart, illustrated by Barbara Reid (New York: Scholastic, 1995). Reid's plasticine illustrations are a wonderful accompaniment to Bogart's text, which features a traveling grandmother and her granddaughter. The grandmother always asks, "What would you have me bring?" And her granddaughter gives whimsical answers.

VARIATION:

Use gift bags rather than wrapped boxes.

I Love My Family; My Family Loves Me

AGES: 2–5

ADULT PREPARATION:

1. Send a letter home to the children's families requesting that each send in a family picture.
2. Put all pictures into a large bowl.

PROCEDURES:

1. Select one child to pull a picture out of the bowl.
2. Have children identify their classmate in the picture and then sing this song:

    I Love My Family; My Family Loves Me

    (notes are given for each syllable and range from middle C to G above middle C)

    I love my family;

    C•C•D•E•E•G

    My family loves me.

    G•F•F•D•D•C

    This is [child's name]'s family,

    C•C•[C•D]•E•E•G

    As happy as can be.

    G•F•F•D•D•C

    Who's in [his or her] family?

    C•C•[D]•E•E•G

    Let's count and see,

    F•D•D•C

    one, two, [count up to the total number in the family].

    There are [number] in [his or her] family,

    C•C•[C]•C•[D]•E•E•G

    As happy as can be.

    G•F•F•D•D•C

3. Continue until each child has had a turn to pull a picture out of the bowl.

DEVELOPMENTAL GOALS:

- ✂ To understand the concept of families
- ✂ To enhance rational counting skills

LEARNING OBJECTIVE:

Using pictures, the children will participate in a counting song about families.

MATERIALS:

Family letter (Appendix B, Letter 1)
Pictures of children's families
Large bowl

continued

I Love My Family; My Family Loves Me continued

Note: Wait to do this activity when all children have brought in a picture. Feelings will get hurt if every child does not get a turn to have his or her family in the song.

EXPANSIONS:

✄ Read *Chicken Sunday* by Patricia Polacco (New York: Scholastic, 1992), in which three children work together to earn their grandma a gift by making Ukrainian eggs.

✄ Read *Grandfather's Journey* by Allen Say (Boston: Houghton Mifflin, 1993). A winner of the Caldecott Award, this author-illustrator retells the story of his grandfather's love for his two homes: California and Japan.

Instruments in a Bag

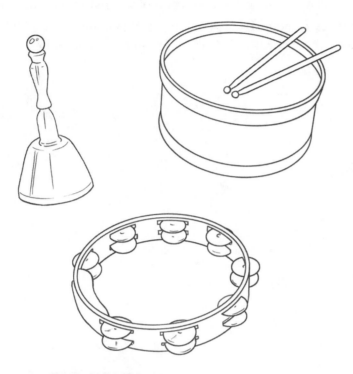

ADULT PREPARATION:

1. Put instruments into a large bag or a pillowcase that children cannot see through.

PROCEDURES:

1. Hold up each instrument for children to identify. (If time allows, pass each instrument around the circle.)
2. Put the instruments back into the bag.
3. Reach inside the bag and play one of the instruments.
4. Ask the children to guess which instrument you played.
5. Repeat steps 3–4 until all of the instruments' sounds have been identified.

Note: The number of instruments put into the bag depends on the age and attention span of the children. For younger children, use fewer instruments. Also, there must be room in the bag to play each instrument. Use more than one bag, if necessary.

continued

AGES: 3–5

DEVELOPMENTAL GOALS:

✂ To enhance auditory discrimination

✂ To increase vocabulary

LEARNING OBJECTIVE:

Using a pillowcase and musical instruments, the children will identify sounds with only their sense of hearing.

MATERIALS:

Large bag or pillowcase
Instruments
   (e.g., tambourine, triangle, rhythm sticks, bells, small drum)

Instruments in a Bag continued

EXPANSIONS:

✂ Take turns using these instruments and other rhythm instruments.

✂ Read *Lentil* by Robert McCloskey (New York: Viking Press, 1940). Lentil saves the day with his harmonica, in this classic tale.

Jack and Jill

AGES: 3–5

DEVELOPMENTAL GOALS:

✂ To develop patience by taking turns

✂ To role-play

LEARNING OBJECTIVE:

Using two pails and the nursery rhyme "Jack and Jill," the children will take turns acting out a nursery rhyme.

MATERIALS:

Two plastic pails (both of the same size)

ADULT PREPARATION:

1. Place pails on the floor in the group time area.

PROCEDURES:

1. Ask the children, "What is a crown?"
2. Explain that in the nursery rhyme "Jack and Jill," *crown* means "head."
3. Select two children to act out the nursery rhyme.
4. Give each child a plastic pail to hold as they walk in place.
5. Lead the group in saying the nursery rhyme as "Jack" and "Jill" act it out: "Jack and Jill went up the hill to fetch a pail of water. Jack fell down and broke his crown, and Jill came tumbling after."
6. Ask the children, "What would happen if *we* had water in the pail?"
7. Repeat, giving other children a turn to act out the rhyme.

continued

55

Jack and Jill continued

Note: You may want to recite the rhyme first, with all the children, and then break the class into smaller groups to act out the roles of Jack and Jill. Make sure to have engaging, self-regulating activities for other children who are waiting their turns.

EXPANSIONS:

✄ Put a small amount of water in one pail. Have the children pick up both pails, and discuss which one is heavier.

✄ Read other nursery rhymes from Sylvia Long's *Mother Goose* (San Francisco: Chronicle Books, 1999).

VARIATION:

Replace Jack and Jill's names with the names of children acting out the parts.

Kangaroo Hop

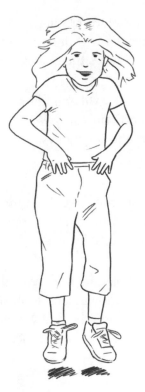

AGES: 3–5

DEVELOPMENTAL GOALS:

- ✂ To improve large muscle coordination
- ✂ To increase the ability to maintain balance

LEARNING OBJECTIVE:

Using pictures of animals, the children will hop like kangaroos and imitate other animal sounds.

MATERIALS:

Newspapers
Magazines
Scissors
Laminating machine and film, or clear contact paper

ADULT PREPARATION:

1. Cut out pictures of animals from magazines and newspaper—a variety of animals that are familiar to children, such as a bird, a fish, a dog, a cat, and a kangaroo.
2. Laminate the pictures.

PROCEDURES:

1. Show the children the picture of a kangaroo. Ask, "How does a kangaroo move?"
2. Have the children hop in place.
3. Show the children pictures of the other animals.
4. Ask, "What sounds do these animals make?" (Bird—tweet, tweet; fish—glub, glub; dog—woof, woof; cat—meow, meow)
5. Tell the children, "When you see the picture of the kangaroo, you will hop. When you see a picture of another animal, you will stop hopping and make that animal's noise."
6. Show children the pictures in random order, showing the kangaroo picture more frequently than the others.

continued

Kangaroo Hop continued

EXPANSIONS:

✂ Read *Zoo Parade!* by Harriet Ziefert (Maplewood, NJ: Blue Apple Books, 2003), which explores the way different animals walk, including the kangaroo, and invites the children to move that way, too.

✂ Read *Joey Kangaroo* by Patricia K. Miller and Iran L. Seligman (New York: Holt, Rinehart and Winston, 1963). This book contains great facts about kangaroos and their joeys.

VARIATIONS:

✂ Explain to children that kangaroos have different hops. They may hop slowly or quickly; they may make large hops or small hops. Then have children hop forward, sideways, in big hops, small hops, and so on.

✂ Show the children an animal picture, then have them move as that animal does. Tell them to stop moving and look at you when they hear you ring a bell. They will then see that you are holding a picture of a different animal, and they should move like that animal until you ring the bell again.

Kind King Kenneth

AGES: 2½–5

DEVELOPMENTAL GOALS:

✂ To introduce the sound of *k*

✂ To increase vocabulary

LEARNING OBJECTIVE:

While wearing crowns, the children will sing a song together.

MATERIALS:

Construction paper
Stapler and staples
Glue
Scissors
Marker

ADULT PREPARATION:

1. Using construction paper, cut crowns to fit the children's heads.
2. Cut various colors of construction paper into small shapes.

PROCEDURES:

1. Have the children glue paper shapes on their crowns, then label the crowns with their names.
2. Allow the crowns to dry.
3. The children will sing the following song while wearing their crown.

   Kind King Kenneth

   (sung to the tune of "Good King Wenceslas")

   Kind King Kenneth kicked the can,

   From Kiawah to Kansas.

   He ate kiwi on a kabob

   While he played the keyboard.

   Kind King Kenneth kept a kayak

continued

Kind King Kenneth continued

Hidden in the kudzu.
He would keep it hidden there
Until he came back from Kansas.

Note: Kiawah, South Carolina, is on the Atlantic coast; kudzu is a fast-growing vine that covers everything in its path.

EXPANSION:

Read *May I Bring a Friend?* by Beatrice Schenk de Regniers (New York: Atheneum, 1964), in which a boy is invited to the king and queen's house and asks to bring a friend with him.

Kookaburra and Koala

AGES: 2–5

DEVELOPMENTAL GOALS:

- ✂ To delight in movement and music
- ✂ To move rhythmically, with a group

LEARNING OBJECTIVE:

Using their bodies, the children will walk to the beat of a song.

MATERIALS:

None needed

ADULT PREPARATION:

1. Clear an area for the group to move in a large circle.

PROCEDURES:

1. Have the children join hands in a circle.
2. Have the children move clockwise as they sing the following song:

   Kookaburra and Koala

   (sung to the tune of "Row, Row, Row Your Boat")

   Kookaburra and Koala went to the park one day.

   It was sunny; they were excited, that they got to play.

   Kookaburra and Koala climbed to the top of the slide.

   Down, down, down they went, and landed in a pile.

Note: A kookaburra is a bird that is native to Australia.

EXPANSION:

Read *Koala Lou* by Mem Fox (San Diego, CA: Harcourt Brace Jovanovich, 1988). Koala Lou misses having all of her mother's attention after her brothers and sisters are born, and she plans to participate in the Bush Olympics in an attempt to regain her mother's love.

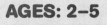

AGES: 2–5

DEVELOPMENTAL GOALS:

- ✂ To grasp number concepts
- ✂ To improve muscle coordination

LEARNING OBJECTIVE:

Using black plastic or paper cups and paper coins, the child will recognize numbers and count objects, using rational counting.

MATERIALS:

Black cups (from discount store)
Yellow construction paper
Scissors
Laminating machine and film, or clear contact paper
White sticky labels, or masking tape
Marker

Leprechaun's Gold

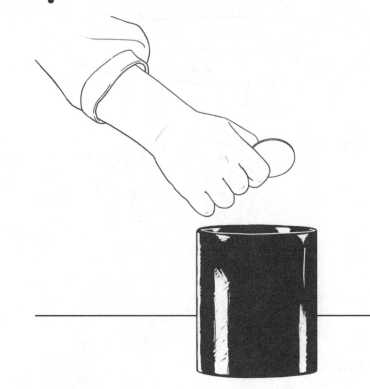

ADULT PREPARATION:

1. Cut yellow circles approximately 2" in diameter out of construction paper.
2. Laminate the circles.
3. Use masking tape on the back of the circles to hide these "coins" around the room.
4. Write a number on white sticky labels or masking tape (suggestions: use the number 2 for two-year-olds, 5 for three-year-olds, 10 for four-year-olds, and 12 for five-year-olds).
5. Stick the numbered labels on the black cups.

PROCEDURES:

1. Tell the children, "Leprechauns are pretend creatures who hide their gold where they think no one can find it. Today we're going to pretend to be leprechauns and gather our gold." Tell children that leprechauns are quiet as they move, because they don't want anyone to hear them.
2. Give each child a black cup.

continued

Leprechaun's Gold continued

3. Ask the children to identify the number on the cup.

4. Children search through the room and count the coins as they find them, placing them in their cups.

5. Once the children have collected the number of coins equal to the number on their cups, they return to the group area.

6. When all children have returned to the group area, have children recount the coins in their cups.

EXPANSION:

Read *Jack and the Leprechaun* by Ivan Robertson (New York: Random House, 2000). Information regarding the St. Patrick celebration is woven throughout the book, which tells the story of Jack Mouse's visit to his cousin in Ireland.

Lily Pad Hop

AGES: 3–5

DEVELOPMENTAL GOALS:

✂ To recognize numbers

✂ To develop large-muscle skills

LEARNING OBJECTIVE:

Using paper lily pads, the children will hop in numerical order.

MATERIALS:

Green construction paper
Lily pad pattern (Appendix A23)
Scissors
Laminating machine and film, or clear contact paper
Masking tape

ADULT PREPARATION:

1. Copy and cut out 11 lily pads from green construction paper.
2. Write numbers 0–10 on the lily pads.
3. Laminate the lily pads.
4. Place them in a circle on the floor in sequential order from 0–10.
5. Place masking tape on the back of each lily pad to prevent it from sliding.

PROCEDURES:

1. Show children the lily pads and ask them to identify the numbers.
2. Have children line up behind the lily pad labeled 0.
3. Have children hop from lily pad to lily pad in numerical order, according to the numbers on the lily pads.
4. When they have all reached lily pad 10, change the order of the lily pads.

continued

64

Lily Pad Hop continued

5. Have the children continue hopping to the lily pads in sequential order by finding the next number before hopping, because the lily pads are no longer laid out in numerical order.

EXPANSION:

Read *Jump, Frog, Jump!* by Robert Kalan (New York: Greenwillow Books, 1981). Children will enjoy repeating, "Jump, frog, jump!" as the frog escapes perilous situations.

DEVELOPMENTAL GOALS:

✂ To increase creativity

✂ To expand vocabulary

LEARNING OBJECTIVE:

Using kazoos, the children will say the nursery rhyme "Little Boy Blue, Come Blow Your Horn" and act it out.

MATERIALS:

One empty toilet paper roll per child

One rubber band per child

Wax paper

Markers

Scissors

Little Boy Blue, Come Blow Your Horn

ADULT PREPARATION:

1. Cut a wax paper circle for each child, approximately 2" wider than the diameter of an empty toilet paper roll.

PROCEDURES:

1. Have the children color their empty toilet paper rolls, with markers.

2. With the tip of the scissors, poke a hole, ¼" in diameter approximately 1½" from one end of each child's toilet paper roll.

3. Wrap a wax paper circle around the end of each toilet paper roll on the end near the hole, securing the wax paper to the roll with a rubber band. Be careful not to cover up the hole with the wax paper.

4. Have children say "Little Boy Blue" with you, and then blow their horns when instructed:

Little Boy Blue

Little Boy Blue, come blow your horn; [*toot kazoos*]

The sheep's in the meadow, [*toot kazoos*]

The cow's in the corn. [*toot kazoos*]

Where is the boy who looks after the sheep? [*hold fingers to mouths, miming "shhh"*]

He's under the haystack, fast asleep. [*fold hands together, laying heads on hands as though sleeping*]

5. Repeat rhyme, having the children vary the way that they blow their horns (loud, soft, long, short).

EXPANSION:

Read excerpts from Tomie de Paola's *Mother Goose* (New York: G. P. Putnam's Sons, 1985).

Make Bread with the Little Red Hen

ADULT PREPARATION:

1. Wash hands.
2. Grease one bowl lightly with butter.
3. Dampen a cloth with water.
4. Set out ingredients and supplies for making bread.

PROCEDURES:

1. Read *The Little Red Hen* to the children.
2. Following the story, have the adult and children wash their hands.
3. The adult will wash the table; the children will sit around the table.
4. Let the children take turns to add and mix the following ingredients to make approximately 10 individual servings of bread:

   3 packages of yeast (6 teaspoons) mixed in 1 cup warm water

   6 tablespoons of sugar

   2 tablespoons of salt

   4 tablespoons of softened butter

   3½ cups of warm water

   13–15 cups of flour, add slowly and mix well.
5. Divide the dough and allow all children to help knead it on a clean foam plate that is lightly dusted with flour. The bread should be kneaded until it is elastic and no longer sticky.
6. The adult will collect the dough and mix it together into one large ball.
7. Put the dough back in the large greased bowl and cover it loosely with a damp cloth.
8. Let the dough rise until it doubles in size (1–1½ hours).
9. Punch the dough down and let it rise again for 30 minutes.
10. The adult will lightly grease individual bread pans with butter.
11. Divide the dough again, making one ball for each child.
12. Have children wash their hands again, and then let them shape the dough and put it into their individual bread pans.

AGES: 3–5

DEVELOPMENTAL GOALS:

- To appreciate literature
- To observe transformations

LEARNING OBJECTIVE:

Using the book *The Little Red Hen* and milk, yeast, flour, sugar, a bowl, and measuring utensils, the child will hear a story and then make bread.

MATERIALS:

The Little Red Hen by Barry Downard (New York: Simon & Schuster, 2004)
Flour
Yeast
Sugar
Water
Measuring cups
Measuring spoons
Butter
Foam plates
Cloth
Two large bowls
Individual-loaf-size aluminum bread pans

continued

Make Bread with the
Little Red Hen continued

13. Allow dough to rise one more time (1–1½ hours).

14. Bake the bread at 375° for approximately 30 minutes (or until golden brown). Or you may cover the bread pans with foil and let the children take them home to bake (be sure to include written instructions).

(This recipe was provided by Betty Somermeyer of Mt. Pleasant, Iowa.)

Note: This recipe makes four full-size loaves of bread.

VARIATIONS:

✂ Make cake with Paul Galdone's *The Little Red Hen* (New York: Clarion Books, 1973).

✂ Make breakfast with Alan Garner's *The Little Red Hen.* (New York: DK Publishing, 1997).

Milk the Cow

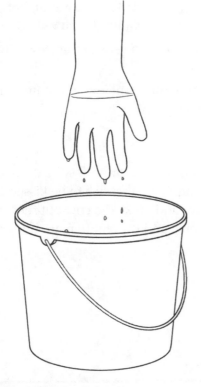

AGES: 3–5

DEVELOPMENTAL GOALS:

✄ To role-play life situations

✄ To improve social skills by taking turns

LEARNING OBJECTIVE:

Using a cow cutout, a glove, milk, and a bucket, the children will pretend to milk a cow.

MATERIALS:

Cow pattern (Appendix A24)
Opaque projector
Large poster board
Pencil
Markers or crayons
Utility knife
Latex glove (use plastic if any children are allergic to latex)
Push pin
Masking tape
Child-size chair
Bucket
Milk or diluted white paint
Plastic sheet

ADULT PREPARATION:

1. Using the cow pattern and the opaque projector, trace a large cow onto poster board.

2. Use a utility knife to cut a slit where the udder would be (to slip the glove through).

3. Color the cow with markers or crayons.

4. Tape the cow to the back of a child-size chair.

5. Place a plastic sheet on the floor and put the cow and chair on the sheet.

6. Place a bucket under the cow. (If a bucket is too tall, use a dish pan.)

7. Use a push pin to poke a hole in each fingertip of the glove.

8. Fill the glove half full of milk or diluted white paint.

9. Slip the opening of the glove through the slit in the cow. (You must retain a secure hold on the opening of the glove throughout the procedure.)

continued

Milk the Cow continued

PROCEDURES:

1. Have the children sit in a semicircle at least four feet away from the cow to ensure they do not get squirted with milk or paint.

2. Explain that milk comes from cows, and that cows are milked by pulling on their udders.

3. Invite the children to take turns pulling on the fingers of the udder while pointing the fingers into the bucket.

EXPANSION:

Read *Kiss the Cow!* by Phyllis Root (Cambridge, MA: Candlewick Press, 2000). Mama May has a magic cow that has to be kissed after being milked. Annalisa sneaks out and milks the cow but refuses to kiss her. Now the cow won't give milk, and the children are hungry!

Mirror, Mirror, What Do I See?

AGES: 3–5

DEVELOPMENTAL GOALS:

- ✄ To develop self-esteem
- ✄ To learn others' names

LEARNING OBJECTIVE:

Using an unbreakable mirror, the children will recite a rhyme while learning classmates' names.

MATERIAL:

Unbreakable mirror

ADULT PREPARATION:

1. Clear an area for group time.

PROCEDURES:

1. Have children sit on the floor in a circle.
2. The adult will model what the children will do by looking into the mirror and reciting, "Mirror, mirror, what do I see? I see [adult's name] looking at me."
3. Pass the mirror to a child.
4. That child looks into the mirror and says, "Mirror, mirror, what do I see? I see [that child's name] looking at me."
5. Have the children pass the mirror around the circle, with each child taking a turn. The entire group may say the rhyme with each child.

continued

Mirror, Mirror, What Do I See? continued

EXPANSIONS:

✂ Cut the center out of a paper plate and staple a tongue depressor to the bottom of the plate. Have the child hold this as though holding a mirror and then turn and look at the next child. The first child then recites the rhyme but inserts the other child's name as the person seen through the "mirror."

✂ Read *I Went Walking* by Sue Williams (New York: Trumpet Club, 1989). A child goes for a walk and hears, "What did you see?" Children will enjoy repeating this repetitive phrase with the reader.

Moon Walk

AGES: 3–5

DEVELOPMENTAL GOALS:

- ✂ To role play
- ✂ To develop large-muscle skills

LEARNING OBJECTIVE:

Using sponges and masking tape, the children will pretend to walk on the moon.

MATERIALS:

Large rectangular sponges (two for each child)
Masking tape
Block

ADULT PREPARATION:

1. Clear a large area for walking.

PROCEDURES:

1. Hold a block in your hand.
2. Ask the children, "What will happen if I drop this block?"
3. Drop the block. Explain to the children that the block falls to the floor because the earth's gravity pulls it, and that the moon has less gravity than the earth.
4. Strap sponges to the bottom of one shoe belonging to each child, using masking tape.
5. Invite the children to walk around.
6. Ask, "How do your feet feel different?"
7. Strap a sponge to each child's other shoe and invite them to walk around again.

continued

Moon Walk continued

8. Tell the children that when astronauts walk on the moon, they feel lighter and bounce as they walk, because the moon has less gravity.

EXPANSION:

Read *I'll Catch the Moon* by Nina Crews (New York: Greenwillow Books, 1996). A photo collage explores a girl's fantasy of climbing to the moon.

Name Game

ADULT PREPARATION:

1. Take a photo of each child, focusing on the child's face.

PROCEDURES:

1. Hold up one child's picture.
2. Ask the group, "Who is this?"
3. If a child answers, "Me," prompt the group to give the child's name.
4. Write the child's first name on an index card.
5. Repeat steps 1–4 with all the children's pictures.
6. Lay the pictures in a row.
7. Hold up a name card.
8. Ask the children, "Whose name is this?"
9. If a child answers, "Mine," prompt the group to give the child's name.
10. Invite the child to put the name card under his or her picture.
11. Repeat steps 7–10 with all the children's name cards.

EXPANSIONS:

✂ Once first names have been learned, you may add last names. Four-year-olds may also spell their names.

✂ Read *A Perfect Name* by Charlene Costanzo (New York: Dial, 2002), in which mother and father hippopotamuses consider names for their beautiful daughter. They must quickly choose a name before her naming ceremony begins.

VARIATION:

Use the pictures or name cards as a means of visual transition to call individual children to an activity, to wash up, or to snack.

AGES: 3–5
AGE: 2 (only recognize pictures)

DEVELOPMENTAL GOALS:

✂ To identify members of the group
✂ To recognize names

LEARNING OBJECTIVE:

Using photos and name cards, the children will learn their classmates' names.

MATERIALS:

Individual pictures of children
Index cards
Marker

Nose Knows

AGES: 3–5

DEVELOPMENTAL GOALS:

✂ To improve olfactory discrimination skills

✂ To identify scents

LEARNING OBJECTIVE:

Using film canisters, cotton balls, spices, and liquid flavoring, the children will identify smells.

MATERIALS:

Four 35 mm film canisters with lids
Nail and hammer, or pointed scissors
Cotton balls
Ground cinnamon
Liquid vanilla flavoring
Liquid strawberry flavoring
Lemon juice

ADULT PREPARATION:

1. Empty four film canisters.

2. Make a hole in the center of each film canister cap, either with a hammer and nail or with scissors.

3. Put ground cinnamon in the first canister, with a cotton ball on top of the spice to prevent it from spilling out.

4. Put a cotton ball in each of the remaining canisters.

5. Pour liquid flavoring on the cotton balls: vanilla flavoring on one, lemon juice on the second, and strawberry on the third.

6. Snap the lids on the canisters.

7. Check to make sure the scent is identifiable through the hole in the cap. If you are unable to smell the scent, you may want to add more of the spice or flavoring to the canister.

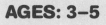

continued

Nose Knows continued

PROCEDURES:

1. Have the children sit in a semicircle.

2. Pass the first spice around the circle, giving each child an opportunity to smell the spice through the hole in the cap.

3. When each child in the group has smelled the first spice, ask the children to guess the identity of the spice.

4. Repeat steps 2–3 until all four scents have been identified.

Obstacle Course

AGES: 3–5
AGE: 2 (only use the numbers 1–5)

DEVELOPMENTAL GOALS:

✂ To identify numbers

✂ To sequence by numbers

LEARNING OBJECTIVE:

Using numbered signs, chairs, and tables, the children will travel through an obstacle course.

MATERIALS:

Construction paper
Scissors
Masking tape
Markers
Chairs
Tables

ADULT PREPARATION:

1. Cut construction paper into 6" squares, making 20 squares.
2. Make two sets of numbers 1–10, by writing the numbers on the squares.
3. Tape one set of numbered squares around the room (tape them to chairs, on the floor under tables, and so on). Do not put them in numerical sequence; mix them up.
4. Set the other set of numbered squares where the children meet for group time.

PROCEDURES:

1. Have the children sit in a semicircle.
2. Hold up the numbers, in numerical order.
3. Ask the children to identify the numbers as they are held up.

continued

Obstacle Course continued

4. Tell the children that they are to find the numbers taped around the room and touch the numbers in order. First they must find 1, and then 2, and so on. If the numbers are under a table, they must climb under the table to the other side in order to continue.

5. When the children have touched all the numbers in order, they will meet back at the designated group area.

6. When all children have completed the obstacle course, they may go through again if desired.

VARIATION:

The paper may be cut into other shapes instead of squares; for instance, during a dinosaur unit, you may want to use dinosaur shapes for the signs.

O

DEVELOPMENTAL GOALS:

✂ To recognize colors

✂ To develop self-esteem

LEARNING OBJECTIVE:

Using a flannel board and felt tree, fruit, sky, and monkeys, the children will help tell a story with pictures.

MATERIALS:

Monkey pattern (Appendix A25)
Tree pattern (Appendix A26)
Circle
Red, green, blue, and brown felt
Flannel board

One Little Monkey, Sitting in a Tree

ADULT PREPARATION:

1. Using the monkey pattern, make one red, one green, one blue, and three brown felt monkeys.
2. Using the tree pattern, make a felt tree with a brown trunk and green leaves.
3. Draw a circle to make a piece of red felt fruit.
4. Cut a blue strip of felt for the sky.

PROCEDURES:

1. Have the children take turns putting appropriate flannel pieces on the flannel board as you read the following story.

One Little Monkey, Sitting in a Tree

One little monkey, sitting in a tree, looked at the leaves and wished she were green. Along came a magic fairy who said, "Poof! You are green, but things are not always as they seem."

One little green monkey, sitting in a tree, wanted to play, but watched her friends walk by. She could not be seen since she looked like a leaf.

One little green monkey, sitting in a tree, looked at the fruit and wished she were red. Along came a magic fairy who said, "Poof! You are red, but things often don't match what is in your head."

One little red monkey, sitting in a tree, wanted to play but watched her friends walk by. She could not be seen, since she looked like a piece of fruit.

One little red monkey, sitting in a tree, looked at the sky and wished she were blue. Along came a magic fairy who said, "Poof! You are blue, but things are often not better new."

One little blue monkey, sitting in a tree, wanted to play but watched her friends walk by. She could not be seen, since she looked like the sky.

One little blue monkey, lonely as can be, looked at her friends and wished she were brown. Along came a magic fairy who said, "Poof! You are brown. Now things are back to how they belong."

continued

80

One Little Monkey, Sitting in a Tree continued

EXPANSIONS:

✄ Read *Caps for Sale* by Esphyr Slobodkina (New York: W. R. Scott, 1947). In this classic book, a peddler who sells caps loses them all to monkeys. How will he get them back?

✄ Read *Five Little Monkeys Jumping on the Bed* by Eileen Christelow (New York: Houghton Mifflin, 1989). This standard chant has a surprise ending for the monkeys' mom.

VARIATION:

Cut monkeys from construction paper, and put magnets on the back to use on a magnetic board.

DEVELOPMENTAL GOALS:

✂ To develop observation skills

✂ To count by rote

LEARNING OBJECTIVE:

Using a 35 mm film canister, water, and Alka-Seltzer® tablets, the children will take turns making a rocket.

MATERIALS:

35 mm film canister with a tightly fitting lid
Child-size pitcher
Water
Alka-Seltzer® tablets
Small bowl
Paper towels

One, Two, Three, Blastoff!

ADULT PREPARATION:

1. Put water in a child-size pitcher.
2. Break Alka-Seltzer® tablets into quarters.
3. Place tablet pieces in a small bowl.
4. Place paper towels on table.

PROCEDURES:

1. The children will take turns using the child-size pitcher to fill a film canister half full of water.
2. Have a child put one or two pieces of an Alka-Seltzer® tablet into the canister.
3. Snap the lid on the canister, making sure it is on tight.

continued

One, Two, Three, Blastoff! continued

4. Have a child turn the canister upside down, resting the lid on paper towels, and then stand back.

5. Count with the children, "One, two, three . . ." until the canister breaks free of the lid and shoots into the air.

6. Repeat steps 1–5 giving other children a turn to set off the "rocket."

Note: Children and adults should stand back from the canister to ensure that neither the canister nor the spray will hit them on liftoff.

EXPANSION:

Read *Dmitri, the Astronaut* by Jon Agee (New York: HarperCollins, 1996). Dmitri has been on the moon for so long that when he returns to earth, no one knows who he is.

Parachute with Beach Ball

DEVELOPMENTAL GOALS:

✂ To develop the large muscles

✂ To participate in a group activity

LEARNING OBJECTIVE:

Using a parachute, the children will bounce a beach ball.

MATERIALS:

Parachute (use a sheet if a parachute is not available)

Beach ball

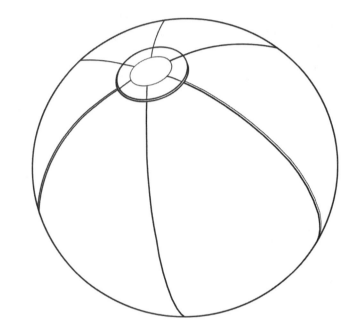

ADULT PREPARATION:

1. Clear a large area for this activity.
2. Blow up the beach ball.
3. Check the parachute. Those without a hole in the center work better, unless the hole is smaller than the beach ball. If the hole is larger than the beach ball, pin it shut so the ball will not fall through the hole.

PROCEDURES:

1. Spread the children out in a circle around the parachute; try to space the children evenly apart.
2. Have each child hold onto a section of the parachute.

continued

84

Parachute with Beach Ball continued

3. Put the beach ball in the center of the parachute.

4. Have the children lift the parachute up and down, moving together. The beach ball will bounce with the movement of the parachute.

EXPANSION:

Read *Beach Ball* by Peter Sis (New York: Greenwillow Books, 1990). Mary's beach ball is blown away in this nearly wordless picture book. Each set of pages that the ball rolls through gives children an opportunity to search for colors, shapes, opposites, and so on.

Pet Classification

DEVELOPMENTAL GOALS:

- ✄ To introduce graphing
- ✄ To classify objects

LEARNING OBJECTIVE:

Using paper, masking tape, and pictures of pets, the children will classify and graph pets by type.

MATERIALS:

Family letter (Appendix B, Letter 2)
Photographs of children's pets
Magazine pictures of pets
Large sheet of paper
Yardstick
Masking tape
Marker

ADULT PREPARATION:

1. Send a family letter home asking families to have the children bring in pictures of their pets or, if they do not have pets, magazine pictures of pets they like.
2. Using a yardstick, draw columns on a large sheet of paper.
3. Tape the sheet of paper on the wall.

PROCEDURES:

1. Discuss what types of pets the children have.
2. Write the types of pets on the bottom of the columns of the large sheet of paper (e.g., dogs, cats, fish, lizards, rabbits).
3. Ask the children who have dogs to tape pictures of their dogs in the column above the word *dog*.
4. Repeat step 3 with other types of pets.
5. When all of the pet pictures have been taped on the paper, count the number of animals in each column.
6. Write the number of pets in each column, either at the bottom of the column or above the top picture of each column.

EXPANSIONS:

- ✄ Discuss which type of pet has the most (least) number of animals.
- ✄ Read *Pet Show* by Ezra Jack Keats (New York: Macmillan, 1972), in which Archie's cat is missing when it's time for the pet show.

Pizza Song

ADULT PREPARATION:

1. Cut a poster board in a circle and color it like a pizza.
2. Using markers, copy the words to "Pizza Song" in large letters on the poster board.

PROCEDURES:

1. Have the children sing the following song as they pretend to flip a pizza in the air:

   Pizza Song

   (created by Kristen Jones; sung to the tune of "Row, Row, Row Your Boat")

   Throw, throw, throw your pizza,

   Up in the air.

   Toss and flip, toss and flip,

   Oops, it's everywhere.

EXPANSION:

Read *Curious George and the Pizza* by Margret Rey and Alan J. Shalleck (Boston: Houghton Mifflin, 1985). This book, in which George and his friend go out to dinner at a pizzeria, consists of just 29 pages of pictures and text, and it usually has only one sentence per page.

AGES: 3–5

DEVELOPMENTAL GOALS:

✄ To develop vocabulary

✄ To increase large muscle development

LEARNING OBJECTIVE:

Using a song poster, the children will sing and act out a song.

MATERIALS:

Poster board
Markers

Popcorn Parachute

AGES: 2½–5

DEVELOPMENTAL GOALS:

- ✂ To develop the large muscles
- ✂ To develop social skills

LEARNING OBJECTIVE:

Using crumpled paper and a parachute, the children will simulate popcorn popping.

MATERIALS:

Scrap paper or copy paper
Parachute or sheet

ADULT PREPARATION:

1. Clear a large area to use the parachute.
2. If the parachute has a hole in the center, pin the hole shut.
3. Lay the parachute flat on the floor.
4. Crumple paper.
5. Put the crumpled paper on the parachute.

PROCEDURES:

1. Space the children evenly around the parachute.
2. Invite the children to hold onto the edge of the parachute with both hands.
3. Help the children work together to lift and lower the parachute, watching the crumpled paper bounce (it will look like popcorn popping in the air).

continued

Popcorn Parachute continued

EXPANSIONS:

✂ Read *Popcorn* by Frank Asch (New York: Parent's Magazine Press, 1979). In this story, Sam Bear stays home alone while his parents go to a Halloween party. Sam's friends come over, and they make so much popcorn that it fills the house!

✂ For older children, read Tomie de Paola's *The Popcorn Book* (New York: Holiday House, 1978), which contains many interesting facts about popcorn.

Popping Popcorn

DEVELOPMENTAL GOALS:

✂ To observe transformations

✂ To develop language skills

LEARNING OBJECTIVE:

Using a sheet, air popper, and popcorn, the children will observe how popcorn kernels are transformed by heat.

MATERIALS:

Hot air popcorn popper
Popcorn kernels
Clean sheet
Extension cord, if necessary
Masking tape

ADULT PREPARATION:

1. Clear a large area and lay a clean sheet on the floor.

2. Place the hot air popcorn popper in the center of the sheet and be sure the cord will reach an electrical outlet. Use an extension cord if necessary.

3. Tape the cord to the carpet, to prevent tripping, but don't plug it in until ready to pop the corn.

PROCEDURES:

1. Invite the children to sit around the outside of the sheet (not on the sheet).

2. Show the children the popcorn kernels and ask, "What are these?"

3. Show the children the air popper and ask, "What is this?"

4. Ask the children, "How do the kernels turn into popcorn?"

continued

Popping Popcorn continued

5. Pour the recommended amount of kernels into the popcorn popper.
6. Plug the popper into the outlet.
7. Collect the popcorn in a bowl to save for a snack.

EXPANSION:

Read the *Popcorn Dragon* by Jane Thayer (New York: Scholastic, 1990), in which Dexter the dragon discovers a talent of making popcorn with his hot, smoky breath.

VARIATION:

After collecting some popcorn in a bowl for a snack, take the lid off the popper, and watch the popcorn erupt like a volcano.

SAFETY PRECAUTION:

Supervise children closely, because popcorn may present a choking hazard.

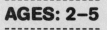

AGES: 2–5

DEVELOPMENTAL GOALS:

✂ To delight in rhythm and motion

✂ To encourage group participation

LEARNING OBJECTIVE:

Using their arms like wings, the children will move to the beat of a song while singing.

MATERIALS:

None needed

Quack, Quack

ADULT PREPARATION:

1. Clear area for group time.

PROCEDURES:

1. Have the children sing the following song, holding their hands in their armpits and flapping their arms like wings each time they sing "quack":

Quack, Quack

(sung to the tune of "Uh Oh, Goes the Little Green Frog")

"Quack, quack," says the little brown duck one day,

C•F•F•G•A•G•F•G•C•C

"Quack, quack," says the little brown duck.

C•F•F•G•A•G•F•G

continued

92

Quack, Quack continued

"Quack, quack," says the little brown duck one day,

C•F•F•G•A•G•F•G•C•C

"Quack, quack," says the little brown duck one day,

C•F•F•G•A•G•F•G•C•C

And his friends say, "Quack, quack," too.

C•C•D•F•E•G•F

EXPANSION:

Read the humorous duck series by Jez Alborough. In *Captain Duck* (New York: HarperCollins, 2003), Duck starts off on a boat trip with his friends but inadvertently leaves without Goat and the extra fuel. In *Duck in the Truck* (New York: HarperCollins, 2000), Duck gets his truck stuck in the muck, and his friends help him out.

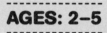

AGES: 2–5

DEVELOPMENTAL GOALS:

✂ To appreciate literature

✂ To practice cooking

LEARNING OBJECTIVE:

Using the nursery rhyme "The Tarts" and ingredients and materials to make tarts, the children will bake a dessert following the story.

MATERIALS:

Plastic tablecloth
Foam plates
Tart shells
Cherry pie filling
Plastic bowls
Cookie sheet
Paper
Permanent marker
Resealable plastic bags
Spoons

Queen of Heart's Tarts

ADULT PREPARATION:

1. Open cans of cherry pie filling and put into plastic bowls.
2. Place a large serving spoon in each bowl.
3. Set out the tart shells, cookie sheet, and plastic tablecloth.

PROCEDURES:

1. Read to the children the following nursery rhyme and then have them repeat it, line by line.

   The Tarts

   The Queen of Hearts
   She made some tarts,
   All on a summer's day;
   The Knave of Hearts,
   He stole the tarts,
   And took them clean away.
   The King of Hearts
   Called for the tarts,
   And beat the Knave full sore.
   The Knave of Hearts
   Brought back the tarts,
   And vowed he'd steal no more.

2. Have the children wash their hands.
3. Spread the plastic tablecloth on the floor and have the children sit around the outside of it (not on it).
4. Give each child a tart shell on a foam plate.
5. Have the children pass the bowls of cherry pie filling around the circle and fill their tart shells.
6. Have the children place their tarts on the cookie sheet.
7. Make a chart of where each child's tart is placed.

continued

94

Queen of Heart's Tarts continued

8. Bake according to directions on the tart shell package.

9. Save for the children's snack or put into resealable plastic bags, label with the children's names, and send home.

EXPANSION:

Read *The Missing Tarts* by B. G. Hennessy (New York: Viking Penguin, 1989), in which various Mother Goose characters help the Queen of Hearts find her missing tarts.

R

Rain Cloud

AGES: 2–5

DEVELOPMENTAL GOALS:

- ✄ To develop vocabulary
- ✄ To participate as a group

LEARNING OBJECTIVE:

Using a song poster, the children will sing a song.

MATERIALS:

Poster board
Permanent marker
String
Hole punch
Cups
Black tempera paint
Blue tempera paint
Water
Spoons
Scissors
Brushes

ADULT PREPARATION:

1. Cut a large cloud shape from a poster board.
2. Put a spoonful of black tempera paint into a cup.
3. Dilute the black tempera paint with a lot of water, enough to create a watery gray.
4. Brush over the cloud shape with the diluted tempera, making the cloud gray.
5. When the cloud shape is dry, write the words to "I'm a Little Rain Cloud" on the cloud in large letters, using a permanent marker.
6. Punch holes along the bottom of the cloud.
7. Cut tear-shaped raindrops out of the poster board scraps.
8. Punch a hole in the top of each raindrop.
9. Using diluted blue tempera paint, paint the raindrops blue.

continued

Rain Cloud continued

10. When they are dry, tie the raindrops to the holes in the poster board so that they dangle from the cloud.

11. Hang the cloud poster in the room.

PROCEDURES:

1. The children will sing the following song:

I'm a Little Rain Cloud

(created by Ashly Landes; sung to the tune of "I'm a Little Teapot")

I'm a little rain cloud:

Puffy and gray.

When I am full, I can rain all day.

Better get your raincoats, your umbrellas, too,

Because if you don't, I will rain on you!

EXPANSION:

Read *Rain, Rain, Everywhere* by Christine Leeson (New York: Scholastic, 2003). In this story, Molly Mouse makes new friends after getting caught in a storm, and they all help each other stay safe.

Ride the Train

DEVELOPMENTAL GOALS:

✂ To promote role playing

✂ To stimulate imagination

LEARNING OBJECTIVE:

Using chairs and tickets, the children will pretend to ride on a train.

MATERIALS:

Chairs
Tickets
Night Train by Caroline Stutson (Brookfield, CT: Roaring Brook Press, 2002)

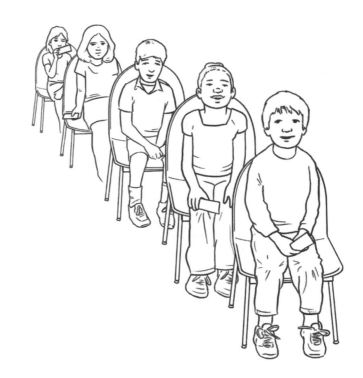

ADULT PREPARATION:

1. Set chairs in rows. Leave room for an aisle to walk between the seats.

PROCEDURES:

1. Have the children sit on the floor.
2. Read the book, *Night Train.*
3. Assign the role of conductor to one of the children.
4. Give each child a ticket.
5. Have the children line up as the conductor calls, "All aboard!"
6. Have the children sit in the chairs after boarding the train.
7. Have the conductor walk down the aisle and collect the tickets from the passengers.

continued

Ride the Train continued

8. As the train starts to move, point out familiar landmarks to the children.

9. Select some children to serve a snack on the train. The snack can be imaginary, or the children may decide to eat their customary snack on the train.

Note: *Night Train* by Caroline Stutson features a rhyming text which is accompanied by Katherine Tillotson's soft illustrations depicting a boy and an adult traveling by train.

VARIATIONS:

✂ Pretend to go on a boat ride, and read *Secret Seahorse* by Stella Blackstone (Cambridge, MA: Barefoot Books, 2004). This book contains colorful collages by Clare Beaton, with a section on the creatures of the coral reef.

✂ Sing "The Wheels on the Bus" and pretend to ride the bus.

✂ At the end of a rainforest unit, decorate the room with toucans, snakes, monkeys, vines, and projects the children have made. Then pretend to go on a safari and look for objects found in the rain forest.

Shape Search

AGES: 2¹/₂–5 (Use fewer shapes with younger children, for instance, two different shapes for two-year-olds, three different shapes for three-year-olds.)

- - - - - - - - - - - - - - - -

DEVELOPMENTAL GOALS:

✂ To identify shapes

✂ To delight in movement and music

LEARNING OBJECTIVE:

Using basic shapes, chairs, and music, the children will march to a beat to find specific shapes on the chairs.

MATERIALS:

Construction paper
Scissors
Chairs
Basket
Music (CD player and CD, or tape and tape player)
Masking tape

ADULT PREPARATION:

1. Cut construction paper into basic shapes. Make one shape for each child.
2. Cut a second set of shapes, identical to the first.
3. Set children's chairs in a circle, with the seats facing outward.
4. Tape the first set of shapes inside the chairs' backs, so that the children can see the shapes as they march around outside the circle.
5. Place the matching shapes in a basket.

PROCEDURES:

1. Ask each child to select a shape from the basket.
2. Play the music, and have the children march around the circle of chairs.

continued

Shape Search continued

3. Stop the music, and have each child find and sit in the chair with the shape matching the one that he or she is holding.

4. Once all children have found their chairs, have them put the shapes back in the basket.

5. Repeat steps 1–4.

Note: Younger children are confused if shapes and colors are mixed, so use the same color for all shapes. If children are to identify colors, use a variety of colors but only one shape.

EXPANSION:

Read *The Shape Detectives (Blue's Clues)* by Angela C. Santomero (New York: Simon & Schuster, 1998). With Blue's help, children can go on a shape hunt.

VARIATION:

Go on a seashell hunt during a beach unit.

AGES: 3–5

DEVELOPMENTAL GOALS:

✂ To participate in role playing

✂ To develop language skills

LEARNING OBJECTIVE:

Using chairs, and sheets, the children will participate in an imaginary sleigh ride.

MATERIALS:

Chairs
Sheets
Masking tape
Book containing the poem (song), "Over the River and Through the Wood" by Lydia Maria Child

Sleigh Ride

ADULT PREPARATION:

1. Set chairs as if they were seats in a large sleigh.
2. Wrap sheets around the outside of the chairs to form the sides of the sleigh, and tape them in place, leaving an opening for the children to enter.

PROCEDURES:

1. Have the children sit in the sleigh.
2. Read "Over the River and Through the Wood" and show children pictures of people riding in sleighs.
3. Ask, "What kind of weather do you need in order to ride in a sleigh?"
4. If the children live in an area where it does not snow, describe how rain turns into snow when it falls through air that is very, very cold.
5. Ask the children, "What kind of clothes would you need to travel in a sleigh?"
6. Ask, "Why did people travel in a sleigh?"
7. Sing the song "Over the River and Through the Woods" while looking at the pictures again.

Note: There are several books based on the poem, "Over the River and Through the Woods," by Lydia Maria Child, which was first published in *Flowers for Children* in 1844. The book, *Over the River and Through the Wood* (New York: Coward-McCann, 1974) contains the entire poem and has eight double pages of wordless illustrations by Brinton Turkle. It also includes a musical score for the poem.

EXPANSION:

Make pumpkin pie and have it for a snack.

Sock Surprise

AGES: 2–5

DEVELOPMENTAL GOALS:

- ✄ To increase tactile discrimination skills
- ✄ To practice taking turns

LEARNING OBJECTIVE:

Using socks and common objects, the children will identify objects by using only their sense of touch.

MATERIALS:

Adult-size socks
Common objects (apple, cup, glue bottle, block, etc.)
Dry erase board, chalkboard, or paper
Dry erase marker, chalk, or marker

ADULT PREPARATION:

1. Place one object in each sock.
2. Loosely knot the end of each sock.

PROCEDURES:

1. Pass the first sock around the circle so the children can feel the object through the sock.
2. When all children have felt the sock, ask, "What do you think is inside?"
3. Write the children's response on the dry erase board, chalkboard, or paper.
4. Untie the sock and remove the object. Were the children correct?
5. Repeat steps 1–4 with other socks.

continued

Sock Surprise continued

EXPANSION:

If the items used in the socks were items found in the classroom, read a book about school, such as *Will I Have a Friend?* by Miriam Cohen (New York: Scholastic, 1967). It is Jim's first day of school, and he wants to find a new friend. The story takes the reader from the beginning to the end of Jim's school day.

Teddy Bears' Picnic

ADULT PREPARATION:

1. Send the family letter home, asking families to have the children bring in their favorite teddy bears or other stuffed animals.

2. Have additional teddy bears or stuffed animals available in case a child does not bring one.

3. Spread a blanket on the floor.

PROCEDURES:

1. Invite each child to find a seat around the blanket. Invite the children to find seats around the outside of the blanket, bringing their teddy bears or stuffed animals with them.

2. Ask each child to introduce his or her special friend.

3. Read aloud *The Teddy Bears' Picnic*.

4. Let children eat their snack with their special friends.

Note: It is beneficial to do activities at the beginning of the year that encourage a transfer of objects from home to school, to help the child become comfortable in the classroom.

AGES: 2–5

DEVELOPMENTAL GOALS:

✂ To acquire self-esteem

✂ To promote emotional development by making a transfer from home to school

LEARNING OBJECTIVE:

Using snack, a blanket, and teddy bears or stuffed animals brought from home, the children will have a picnic.

MATERIALS:

Family letter (Appendix B, Letter 3)
Blanket
Stuffed animals
Snack
The Teddy Bears' Picnic by Jimmy Kennedy (LaJolla, CA: Green Tiger Press, 1983)

Three Billy Goats Gruff

T

AGES: 4–5

DEVELOPMENTAL GOALS:

✂ To appreciate literature

✂ To promote role playing

LEARNING OBJECTIVE:

Using goat horn headbands, a scarf, and a rug, the children will enact a story that is read to them.

MATERIALS:

The Three Billy Goats Gruff by Paul Galdone (New York: Clarion Books, 1973)
Rectangular rug (at least 3' in length) or towel
Three plastic headbands
Scarf
Construction paper
Scissors

ADULT PREPARATION:

1. Using construction paper, cut out 3 pairs of goat horns. Make one pair small, one pair medium size, and the last pair large. The goat horns may be cut in the shape of triangles or narrow crescents.

2. Tape the horns to the headbands.

3. Lay the rug or towel on the floor.

PROCEDURES:

1. Have the children sit in a semicircle facing the rug.

2. Read the book *The Three Billy Goats Gruff*.

continued

Three Billy Goats Gruff continued

3. Have the children take turns playing different roles from the story. The smallest Billy Goat Gruff will wear the headband with the smallest horns; the midsize horns will be worn by the second goat, and the last goat will wear the headband with the largest horns. The child who plays the troll will wear a scarf tied under his or her chin. The rug will be the bridge.

4. Reread the story as the goats and the troll act it out. (Remember, to vary voices: the smaller the goat, the softer and/or higher the voice.)

5. The children watching may help by saying, "Trip, trap, trip, trap" as the goats cross the bridge.

Note: There are many versions of the Three Billy Goats Gruff. Make sure to pre-read the story. Different versions have varying results for the troll. The story may need to be paraphrased so in acting it out the children respond gently to each other. Paul Galdone's book ends with the troll simply being tossed into the river.

VARIATION:

If this story is being read at home to siblings, change the name to reflect the children's last name (e.g., the three billy goats McLarty).

Tiptoe Tapping By the Tulips

AGES: 3–5

DEVELOPMENTAL GOALS:

- ✂ To develop the large muscles
- ✂ To demonstrate cooperative behavior

LEARNING OBJECTIVE:

Using paper tulips and a gardening hat, the children will participate in a movement game.

MATERIALS:

Tulip pattern (Appendix A27)
Paper
Masking tape
Laminator and film, or clear contact paper
Garden hat

ADULT PREPARATION:

1. Copy the tulip pattern, making enough tulips to equal five times the number of children in the group.
2. Tape the tulips to the floor. The first row should contain the same number of tulips as the number of children in the group. The other tulips may be put in additional rows or just scattered over the remaining floor area.

PROCEDURES:

1. Select one child to be the gardener.
2. Have all other children line up, each standing on a tulip in the first row.
3. Have the gardener wear the hat and stand with his or her back turned to the tulips.
4. Say the following chant with the children as they tiptoe toward the gardener: Tell them that at the end of the chant, each child must be standing on a tulip.

Tiptoe Tapping By the Tulips

Tiptoe tapping by the tulips

On tiptoe tapping feet

When the gardener turns around,

On a tulip we'll be sweet.

5. At the end of the chant, the gardener turns around, any child who is not standing on a tulip must return to the first row.
6. The gardener turns his back to the tulips again. The chant and step 5 are repeated until one of the children reaches the gardener. That child will become the gardener, and repeat steps 2–6.

EXPANSION:

Read *Tulips* by Jay O'Callahan (Atlanta, GA: Peachtree Publishers, 1992), in which a mischievous boy always plays tricks on his grandmother and her servants. His grandest prank is planned as a trick on Grandmother's precious tulips.

Toucan's Feathers

AGES: 3–5

DEVELOPMENTAL GOALS:

✂ To identify colors

✂ To develop counting skills

LEARNING OBJECTIVE:

Using feathers, a picture of a toucan, glue, and a number card, the children will search for and count objects.

MATERIALS:

Toucan pattern (Appendix A28)
Paper
Bag of feathers
Number card
Milk cap or lid
Glue

ADULT PREPARATION:

1. Copy and cut out a picture of the toucan.
2. Hide feathers all around the room. Consider the age and attention span of the group. Hide at least two feathers per child.
3. Place glue in a milk cap or lid.

PROCEDURES:

1. Show the children the picture of the toucan.
2. Explain that the toucan has lost his feathers and needs help finding them.
3. Tell the children how many feathers each of them may find, and show the children the number card bearing that number.
4. Rote count to that number.

continued

109

Toucan's Feathers continued

5. The children search for the feathers all at the same time, or divide the children into smaller subgroups.

6. After finding the feathers, the children may dip the feathers in glue and place them on the toucan.

EXPANSION:

Read *Hey Al!* by Arthur Yorinks (New York: Farrar, Straus and Giroux, 1986). In this Caldecott Medal winner, a toucan leads a disenchanted man and his dog to "paradise," where they began to turn into birds. Gratefully, the pair find their way home. As a result of their experience, they began to appreciate their lives.

Trail Ride

ADULT PREPARATION:

1. Using the horse head pattern and tag board, trace or copy and cut out a horse head for each child.

PROCEDURES:

1. Invite the children to decorate their horse heads with markers, crayons, yarn, and glue.
2. Staple each horse head onto one end of an empty wrapping paper tube.
3. Let the glue dry, then pass the horses out to the children.
4. Tell the children to mount, by swinging one leg over the horse.
5. Lead the children in dialogues about and pantomimes of activities such as the following:
   a. Packing for the trail ride
   b. Deciding where to ride
   c. Stopping to let the horses rest
   d. Describing what they see
   e. Herding cattle back to the ranch
   f. Taking care of the horses when the ride is over

EXPANSIONS:

✄ Read *On the Trail with Miss Pace* by Sharon Phillips Denslow (New York: Simon & Schuster, 1995). Miss Pace, a schoolteacher, heads to a ranch in the West for her summer vacation. Imagine her surprise when she finds two of her students already there!

✄ Read *Why Cowboys Sleep with Their Boots On* by Laurie Lazzaro Knowlton (Gretna, LA: Pelican Publishing, 1995). Slim Jim Watkins is a cowboy out on the trail, and he always seems to lose some of his clothes at night to sneaky animals.

AGES: 3–5

DEVELOPMENTAL GOALS:

✄ To develop creativity
✄ To promote role playing

LEARNING OBJECTIVE:

Using horses, children will go on a trail ride.

MATERIALS:

Empty gift wrap tubes
Horse head pattern (Appendix A29)
Tag board
Yarn
Stapler and staples
Markers and crayons
Glue

Umpire and Unicorn

AGES: 2–5

DEVELOPMENTAL GOALS:

✄ To develop vocabulary

✄ To develop the large muscles

LEARNING OBJECTIVE:

Using paper umbrellas as props, the children will move clockwise and sing.

MATERIALS:

Construction paper

Empty paper towel tubes (one for each child)

Scissors

Hot glue gun and glue sticks

Markers or crayons

ADULT PREPARATION:

1. Cut construction paper into large circles.
2. To make umbrellas, hot-glue each circle to one end of an empty paper towel tube.

PROCEDURES:

1. Have the children stand in a circle.
2. Sing the following song with the children, as they hold their umbrellas above their heads and move in a clockwise circle:

   Umpire and Unicorn

   (sung to the tune of "I've Got Something in My Pocket")

   The umpire and the unicorn

   C•F•F•F•F•F•F•F

continued

Umpire and Unicorn continued

Are standing in the rain.

F•G•G•D•D•G

They're looking for umbrellas,

F•E•E•E•E•E•E

While they get soaked with rain.

D•C•C•D•E•F

They ask for my umbrella;

C•F•F•F•F•F•F

I tell them, "I can share."

F•G•G•D•D•G

So we're standing with umbrellas

G•F•E•E•E•E•E•E

In odd-looking pairs.

D•C•D•E•F

EXPANSION:

Read *Big Sarah's Little Boots* by Paulette Bourgeois (New York: Scholastic, 1987). In this story, Sarah loves to splash in the puddles in her favorite yellow boots. Then she thinks that they have shrunk, and she tries to make them grow, just as she has. In the end, she ends up sharing them with her younger brother.

Under the Stars

AGES: 3–5

DEVELOPMENTAL GOALS:

- ✄ To identify shapes
- ✄ To provide visual stimulation

LEARNING OBJECTIVE:

Using glow-in-the-dark stars, the children will identify the basic shapes in which the stars are arranged.

MATERIALS:

Sleeping bags or towels
Peel-and-stick plastic glow-in-the-dark stars
Small battery-operated lantern, if there's no window in the group area
Yardstick

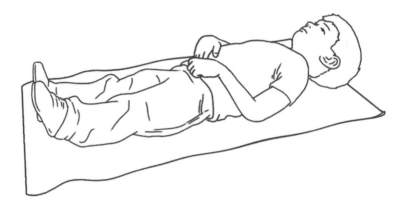

ADULT PREPARATION:

1. Peel and stick the plastic glow-in-the dark stars on the ceiling, placing them in outlines of basic shapes (e.g., squares, triangles, etc.).
2. Lay the sleeping bags or towels in a circle.

PROCEDURES:

1. Have children lie on their backs on the sleeping bags or towels.
2. Turn off the lights. (If there is no window in the room, use a small battery-operated lantern so children are not in total darkness.)
3. Ask the children, "What do you see?"
4. Using a yardstick as a pointer, help the children identify the shapes in which the stars are placed.

EXPANSION:

Read *Stars* by Sarah L. Schuette (Mankato, MN: Capstone Press, 2003). Stars are found all around us, as noted in this book filled with bright illustrations, large text, and a subtext of facts.

Valentine Partners

ADULT PREPARATION:

1. Select pairs of valentine cards. There must be one pair for each pair of children in the group. If there are an odd number of children, the adult will need to participate as a member of the group.

PROCEDURES:

1. Have the children sit in a circle.
2. Holding the basket above the children's heads—the contents out of their eyesight, but not out of their reach (to avoid having them try to select specific cards)—allow each child to take a card.
3. When all children have cards, ask them to stand and hold their cards in front of them, so everyone in the group can see everyone's valentines.
4. Have each child find his or her matching valentine and sit with that other child.
5. If desired, have everyone replace the cards in the basket and repeat steps 2–4.

EXPANSION:

Read *One Zillion Valentines* by Frank Modell (New York: Greenwillow Books, 1982), in which Marvin and Milton make valentines for everyone. What will they do with the extra valentines they made, and who will make valentines for them?

VARIATION:

Hide one set of valentines in the room. Then have children select valentines from the basket and search the room to find cards that match.

AGES: 3–5

DEVELOPMENTAL GOALS:

✂ To match objects
✂ To develop visual discrimination skills

LEARNING OBJECTIVE:

Using valentine cards, children will match like objects.

MATERIALS:

Pairs of valentine cards
Basket

Vegetable Song

AGES: 2–5

DEVELOPMENTAL GOALS:

✂ To expand vocabulary

✂ To recognize nutritious food

LEARNING OBJECTIVE:

Using a song poster, the children will sing and make appropriate motions as they sing.

MATERIALS:

Poster board
Markers
Magazine pictures of vegetables
Rubber cement
Permanent marker

ADULT PREPARATION:

1. Using a poster board and permanent marker, write the words to "Vegetables Are Good for You" in large print.
2. Cut pictures of vegetables out of magazines.
3. Glue the pictures on the poster board.
4. Set the poster where everyone can see it.

PROCEDURES:

1. Ask the children to identify the foods pictured on the song poster.
2. Have the children sing the following song and make the noted motions:

   Vegetables Are Good for You

   (created by Whitney Boykin; sung to the tune of "Mary Had a Little Lamb")

continued

116

Vegetable Song continued

[During first stanza, rub stomach in a circular motion.]

Vegetables are good for you,

Good for you,

Good for you.

Vegetables are good for you,

So eat them every day.

[During second stanza, flex arm muscles.]

They'll make you grow up big and strong,

Big and strong,

Big and strong.

They'll make you grow up big and strong

And keep you healthy, too.

EXPANSION:

Read *The Pea Patch Jig* by Thacher Hurd (New York: Crown Publishers, 1986). This book tells the adventures of Baby Mouse as she explores Farmer Clem's vegetable garden.

Walk the Tightrope

DEVELOPMENTAL GOALS:

✂ To achieve balance

✂ To improve muscle coordination

LEARNING OBJECTIVE:

Using a child's balance beam and an umbrella, the children will pretend to walk a tightrope.

MATERIALS:

Balance beam or masking tape
Child-size umbrella
Chairs

ADULT PREPARATION:

1. Set up the balance beam on lowest setting. If a balance beam is not available, put a long strip of masking tape on the floor.

2. Set out one chair per child, in a row, four feet from the balance beam.

PROCEDURES:

1. Have children sit in the chairs.

2. Have children take turns walking across the balance beam. Spot each child as he or she walks, holding a hand if necessary.

3. After all children have taken turns walking across, give them the option of walking across the beam holding an umbrella. Explain that often a performer in the circus will hold an umbrella while walking the tightrope.

continued

Walk the Tightrope continued

EXPANSION:

Read *Mirette on the High Wire* by Emily Arnold McCully (New York: G. P. Putnam's Sons, 1992). This Caldedcott Medal winner follows Mirette as she learns to walk on the high wire, which brings her joy and leads to the rescue of a legendary performer.

Whose Voice Do I Hear?

DEVELOPMENTAL GOALS:

✂ To increase auditory discrimination skills

✂ To follow directions

LEARNING OBJECTIVE:

Using a tape player and a tape, the children will identify voices.

MATERIALS:

Tape recorder/player and blank tape

ADULT PREPARATION:

1. Using the tape recorder and a blank tape, make a recording of each child repeating a short nursery rhyme or listing some favorite foods. Make the recordings in a quiet spot, out of the hearing range of other children.

PROCEDURES:

1. Play the first voice on the tape for the children, then stop the tape.
2. Ask the children, "Whose voice do you hear?"
3. If the children guess incorrectly, have that child identify his or her own voice.
4. Continue playing the tape until all voices have been identified.

continued

Whose Voice Do I Hear? continued

VARIATION:

Read and record lines from the children's favorite books. Display the books as the tape is played and have the children guess which book the line is from. It is best to use books that have repeating phrases such as "terrible, horrible, no good, very bad day" (from *Alexander and the Terrible, Horrible, No Good, Very Bad Day* by Judith Viorst, New York: Atheneum, 1972).

Who Is Missing?

AGES: 2–5

DEVELOPMENTAL GOALS:

✄ To visually discriminate between objects

✄ To enhance memory

LEARNING OBJECTIVE:

Using a table and a sheet, the children will identify missing group members.

MATERIALS:

Table
Sheet

ADULT PREPARATION:

1. Cover a table with a sheet, using a large enough sheet to hang down to the floor on all sides so that it is not possible to see under the table.

PROCEDURES:

1. Have the children sit in a semicircle on the floor.
2. Select three to six children to stand in front of the group.
3. Ask the group to identify each child by name.
4. Ask the group to close their eyes.
5. Select one of the children standing to hide under the sheet-covered table.
6. Ask the group to open their eyes, then say, "Who is missing?"
7. Give the children two chances to guess the missing person.

continued

Who Is Missing? continued

8. After they guess correctly or have had their two chances, the missing person may emerge from under the table and identify himself or herself.

9. Repeat steps 2–8, choosing other children to stand in front of the group.

Note: If all children want an opportunity to hide under the table and the group is large, select two children at a time to be missing. If the class is small, it is not necessary to have the children stand in a line in front of the group. Simply select a child to hide from the semicircle.

EXPANSION:

Read *Brown Bear, Brown Bear, What Do You See?* by Bill Martin, Jr., (New York: Henry Holt, 1967). This children's classic starts with what Brown Bear sees and ends with what a class of children see.

VARIATION:

Instead of selecting a child to be missing from the persons standing in the center, add something while the others' eyes are closed (e.g., have someone wear a ribbon, or a hat, or hold an object). Ask, "What's different?" or "What has changed?"

Winter Clothes Relay

DEVELOPMENTAL GOALS:

✄ To participate as a team

✄ To coordinate large and small muscles

LEARNING OBJECTIVE:

Using winter coats, hats, and mittens, the children will participate in a relay putting on winter clothes.

MATERIALS:

Chairs
Winter coat (one per team)
Hat (one per team)
Mittens (one pair per team)

ADULT PREPARATION:

1. Collect old winter coats, hats, and mittens. Avoid using what the children currently wear.
2. Divide the children into teams (four is the maximum number to include on a team).
3. Set up a row of chairs for the teams, with one chair for each team.
4. Place a hat, coat, and pair of mittens on each team's chair.
5. Set one chair across from each team's chair. During the relay, the children will circle around these chairs.

PROCEDURES:

1. Have the children stand with their teams, in line behind their team chairs.
2. The first child in each team will put on the team hat, coat, and mittens.

continued

Winter Clothes Relay continued

3. As soon as the first child on each team has on the hat, coat, and mittens, that child will walk to the chair across from his or her team's chair, circle it, and then return to the team chair.

4. On reaching the team chair, the child will take off the hat, coat, and mittens.

5. The next teammate on each team will then put on the winter clothes and repeat steps 2–4.

6. Continue the procedure until all team members have participated.

Note: If children appear to have difficulty staying with their teams, set out a line of chairs for each team.

EXPANSION:

Read *Moe the Dog in Tropical Paradise* by Diane Stanley (New York: G. P. Putnam's Sons, 1992). Moe and his friend suffer through their winter climate until Moe finds a creative way to bring a tropical paradise to his home.

X-Children

DEVELOPMENTAL GOALS:

✂ To recognize the letter X

✂ To follow directions

LEARNING OBJECTIVE:

Using masking tape, the children will form the letter *x*.

MATERIALS:

Masking tape

ADULT PREPARATION:

1. Put masking tape on the floor in the shape of an *x*. Each leg of the *x* should equal the typical height of children in the group.

PROCEDURES:

1. Ask for four volunteers to help make a letter.
2. Have each volunteer lie along the length of one piece of tape, on his or her back with head toward the center of the *x*, arms at his or her side, and legs straight together.
3. Ask the remaining children, "What letter have they formed?"
4. Repeat steps 1–3, giving all children an opportunity to help form an *x*.

EXPANSIONS:

✂ Repeat this process for all letters of the alphabet. Take overhead pictures of the children once each set forms a letter. Develop the pictures and bind them into an alphabet book.

✂ Read an alphabet book such as *Alphabet Under Construction* by Denise Fleming (New York: Scholastic, 2003). This book has wonderful illustrations of mice forming the entire alphabet.

X Marks the Spot

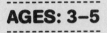

AGES: 3–5

DEVELOPMENTAL GOALS:

- ✂ To follow directions
- ✂ To develop social skills

LEARNING OBJECTIVE:

Using pictures, the children will participate in a treasure hunt.

MATERIALS:

Camera
Masking tape

ADULT PREPARATION:

1. Take photographs of objects in the room (e.g., the mirror in the restroom, the calendar, the block bin or shelf).

2. Going to those same objects, tape one picture of a different object at each spot. The purpose of the photo is to tell the children where to go next (e.g., tape a picture of the calendar on the restroom mirror).

3. Tape all of the photos within reach of the children.

4. The last object that the children go to should be the place where the treasure is found (i.e., the snack table, the playground, the book-shelf where a new book has been added). Place a large X on this location, with masking tape.

5. Keep the photo of the first location that the children are to find (do not tape it anywhere).

PROCEDURES:

1. Tell the children that they are going on a treasure hunt.

2. Hand one child the picture of the first location.

continued

X Marks the Spot continued

3. Tell the child to go to that location to find the next clue and to bring the group a picture that will be found there. If the child is unable to identify the first location from its photo, the group may help.

4. The child then goes to the first location and returns to the group with the photo found there.

5. That child gives the second photo to another child, and the process continues until the last picture is found. Then the entire group finds the treasure together.

Note: Depending on the size of the group, children may be sent in pairs to retrieve the photos.

EXPANSION:

Read *Spot's Treasure Hunt* by Eric Hill (New York: G. P. Putnam's Sons, 2002), in which Spot the dog goes on a treasure hunt. The pages contain flaps that lift to reveal a hidden picture.

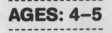

Yellow Yarn Web

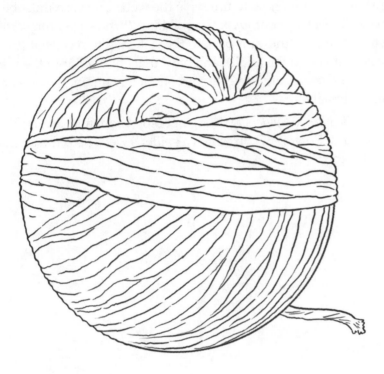

AGES: 4–5

DEVELOPMENTAL GOALS:

- ✂ To coordinate large and small muscles
- ✂ To improve social skills by functioning as part of a group

LEARNING OBJECTIVE:

Using yarn, the children will work together to spin a web.

MATERIALS:

Yellow yarn

ADULT PREPARATION:

1. Roll a skein of yellow yarn into a ball.

PROCEDURES:

1. Show the children the ball of yarn. Ask them, "What color is this yarn?"
2. Hold onto the end of the yarn, then call a child by name and roll the ball of yarn to that child.
3. Have that child hold onto a length of the yarn and call another child's name.
4. While holding tight to the length of yarn, the child holding the yarn rolls the ball to the child whose name was called.
5. The process continues until all children have had a turn.
6. Have the last person to receive the ball of yarn roll it back to the adult who started it.
7. Ask the children, "What does the yarn look like?" (It should resemble a spider's web.)

continued

Yellow Yarn Web continued

EXPANSIONS:

✂ Ask the children how to untangle the web. (The yarn must be rolled back in reverse order.) Ask the children, "Who rolled the yarn to you?" Then roll the yarn back to the last child to receive it (the one who rolled it to the adult), and have that child roll it to the previous child and so on, until the yarn is completely untangled and back into its original ball.

✂ Read *Be Nice to Spiders* by Margaret Bloy Graham (New York: Harper & Row, 1967), in which a spider's webs help the animals at the zoo.

Zoo Ride

DEVELOPMENTAL GOALS:

- ✂ To identify animals
- ✂ To practice role playing

LEARNING OBJECTIVE:

Using chairs and pictures of animals, the children will pretend to take a trip on the bus, to the zoo.

MATERIALS:

Pictures of zoo animals
Masking tape
Chairs

ADULT PREPARATION:

1. Set chairs in rows similar to those on a bus.
2. Tape pictures of zoo animals on the walls throughout the room.

PROCEDURES:

1. Tell the children, "Today we are going to the zoo. You can get on the bus for the ride to the zoo."
2. Children "ride the bus." Once they arrive at the zoo, the adult will explain that everyone has to stay together.
3. Walk together to the first habitat (the first picture), then stop and look at the animal.
4. Ask the children to identify the animal and then discuss the animal (e.g., the giraffe's neck is long because it likes to eat leaves; with a long neck, it can eat the leaves from the tops of the trees).
5. Continue the zoo walk, stopping to see all the animals that are pictured on the walls. Ask the children what they know about the animals, and be prepared to give information on each one.

continued

Zoo Ride continued

6. Help the children use their imagination by pretending to stop, to rest, to have a snack, and so on.

7. When all the habitats have been visited, return to the bus and head home.

EXPANSION:

Read *Zoo-Looking* by Mem Fox (Greenvale, NY: Mondo Publishing, 1996). This book is illustrated with collages and watercolors by Candace Whitman and contains a repetitive phrase that children enjoy saying along with the text.

References

Agee, J. (1996). *Dmitri, the Astronaut*. New York: HarperCollins.

Asch, F. (1979). *Popcorn*. New York: Parent's Magazine Press.

Alborough, J. (2000). *Duck in the Truck*. New York: HarperCollins.

Alborough, J. (2003). *Captain Duck*. New York: HarperCollins.

Bate, L. (1975). *Little Rabbit's Loose Tooth*. New York: Crown Publishers.

Benét, R. & Benét, S.V. (1961). *Johnny Appleseed*. New York: McElderry Books.

Blackstone, S. (2004). *Secret Seahorse*. Cambridge, MA: Barefoot Books.

Blumenthal, N. (1989). *Count-a-saurus*. New York: Scholastic.

Bogart, J. E. (1995). *Gifts*. New York: Scholastic.

Borovsky, P. (1990). *George*. New York: Greenwillow Books.

Bourgeois, P. (1987). *Big Sarah's Little Boots*. New York: Scholastic.

Carle, E. (1969). *The Very Hungry Caterpillar*. New York: Philomel Books.

Carle, E. (1987). *The Tiny Seed*. New York: Simon & Schuster.

Carle, E. (1993). *Today Is Monday*. New York: Scholastic.

Carlson, N. (1997). *ABC, I Like Me!* New York: Penguin.

Child, L. M. (1974). *Over the River and Through the Wood*. New York: Coward-McCann.

Christelow, E. (1989). *Five Little Monkeys Jumping on the Bed*. New York: Houghton Mifflin.

Cohen, M. (1967). *Will I Have a Friend?* New York: Scholastic.

Costanzo, C. (2002). *A Perfect Name*. New York: Dial.

Crews, N. (1996). *I'll Catch the Moon*. New York: Greenwillow Books.

Dallas-Conte', J. (2001). *Cock-a-Moo-Moo*. London: Macmillan Children's Books.

Denslow, S. P. (1995). *On the Trail with Miss Pace*. New York: Simon & Schuster.

de Paola, T. (1978). *The Popcorn Book*. New York: Holiday House.

de Paola, T. (1983). *Sing, Pierrot, Sing*. San Diego: Harcourt Brace Jovanovich.

de Paola, T. (1985). *Mother Goose*. New York: G. P. Putnam's Sons.

de Regniers, B. S. (1964). *May I Bring a Friend?* New York: Atheneum.

Downard, B. (2004). *The Little Red Hen*. New York: Simon & Schuster.

Ehlert, L. (1988). *Planting a Rainbow*. San Diego: Harcourt.

Fleming, D. (2003). *Alphabet Under Construction*. New York: Scholastic.

Florian, D. (1990). *A Beach Day*. New York: Greenwillow Books.

Fox, C. & Fox, D. (2001). *Fire Fighter PiggyWiggy*. Brooklyn, NY: Handprint Books.

Fox, M. (1988). *Koala Lou*. San Diego: Harcourt Brace Jovanovich.

Fox, M. (1996). *Zoo-Looking*. Greenvale, NY: Mondo Publishing.

Galdone, P. (1973). *The Little Red Hen*. New York: Clarion Books.

Galdone, P. (1973). *The Three Billy Goats Gruff*. New York: Clarion Books.

Garner, A. (1997). *The Little Red Hen*. New York: DK Publishing.

Gibbons, G. (2000). *Apples*. New York: Holiday House.

Graham, M. B. (1967). *Be Nice to Spiders*. New York: Harper & Row.

Granowsky, A. (2001). *Colors*. Brookfield, CT: Copper Beech Books.

Hennessy, B. G. (1989). *The Missing Tarts*. New York: Viking Penguin.

Hill, E. (2002). *Spot's Treasure Hunt*. New York: G. P. Putnam's Sons.

Hoff, S. (1958). *Danny and the Dinosaur*. New York: HarperCollins.

Hooper, M. (1985). *Seven Eggs*. New York: Harper & Row.

Hurd, T. (1986). *The Pea Patch Jig*. New York: Crown Publishers.

Johnson, J. (2002). *Are You Ready for Bed?* New York: Scholastic.

Kalan, R. (1981). *Jump, Frog, Jump!* New York: Greenwillow Books.

Keats, E. J. (1972). *Pet Show*. New York: Macmillan.

Kennedy, J. (1983). *The Teddy Bears' Picnic*. LaJolla, CA: Green Tiger Press.

Knowlton, L. L. (1995). *Why Cowboys Sleep with Their Boots On*. Gretna, LA: Pelican Publishing.

Leeson, C. (2003). *Rain, Rain, Everywhere*. New York: Scholastic.

Lionni, L. (1963). *Swimmy*. New York: Scholastic.

Lionni, L. (1994). *An Extraordinary Egg*. New York: Knopf.

Livingston, I. (2003). *Finklehopper Frog*. Berkeley, CA: Tricycle Press.

Lobel, A. (1984). *The Rose in My Garden*. New York: Greenwillow Books.

Long, S. (1999). *Mother Goose*. San Francisco: Chronicle Books.

Martin, B. (1967). *Brown Bear, Brown Bear, What Do You See?* New York: Henry Holt.

McCloskey, R. (1940). *Lentil*. New York: Viking Press.

McCully, E. A. (1992). *Mirette on the High Wire*. New York: G. P. Putnam's Sons.

Miller, P. K. & Seligman, I. L. (1963). *Joey Kangaroo*. New York: Holt, Rinehart and Winston.

Modell, F. (1982). *One Zillion Valentines*. New York: Greenwillow Books.

Most, B. (1978). *If the Dinosaurs Came Back*. San Diego: Harcourt.

Murphy, S. J. (1999). *Super Sand Castle Saturday*. New York: HarperCollins.

O'Brien, J. (2000). *The Farmer in the Dell*. Honesdale, PA: Boyds Mills Press.

O'Callahan, J. (1992). *Tulips*. Atlanta, GA: Peachtree.

Pfister, M. (1995). *Hang On, Hopper!* New York: North-South Books.

Polacco, P. (1992). *Chicken Sunday*. New York: Scholastic.

Reese, B. (1995). *Clowns*. Provo, UT: ARO Publishing.

Rey, M. (1958). *Curious George Flies a Kite*. Boston: Houghton Mifflin.

Rey, M. & Shalleck, A. J. (1985). *Curious George and the Pizza*. Boston: Houghton Mifflin.

Rice, E. (1981). *Benny Bakes a Cake*. New York: Greenwillow Books.

Robbins, K. (1998). *Autumn Leaves*. New York: Scholastic Press.

Robertson, I. (2000). *Jack and the Leprechaun*. New York: Random House.

Root, P. (2000). *Kiss the Cow!* Cambridge, MA: Candlewick Press.

Rylant, C. (1984). *This Year's Garden*. New York: Bradbury Press.

Santomero, A. (1998). *The Shape Detectives (Blue's Clues)*. New York: Simon & Schuster.

Say, A. (1993). *Grandfather's Journey*. Boston: Houghton Mifflin.

Schuette, S. L. (2003). *Stars*. Mankato, MN: Capstone Press.

Shannon, D. (2002). *Duck on a Bike*. New York: Scholastic.

Sirimarco, E. (2000). *At the Orchard*. San Juan Capistrano, CA: Child's World.

Sis, P. (1990). *Beach Ball*. New York: Greenwillow Books.

Slobodkina, E. (1947). *Caps for Sale*. New York: W. R. Scott.

Stanley, D. (1992). *Moe the Dog in Tropical Paradise*. New York: G. P. Putnam's Sons.

Stutson, C. (2002). *Night Train*. Brookfield, CT: Roaring Brook Press.

Thayer, J. (1990). *Popcorn Dragon*. New York: Scholastic.

Thomas, P. (1971). *"Stand Back," Said the Elephant, "I'm Going to Sneeze!"* New York: Lothrop, Lee & Shepard.

Tildes, P. L. (1997). *Gifts*. Watertown, MA: Charlesbridge.

Viorst, J. (1972). *Alexander and the Terrible, Horrible, No Good, Very Bad Day*. New York: Atheneum.

Williams, S. (1989). *I Went Walking*. New York: Trumpet Club.

Yektai, N. (1996). *Bears at the Beach*. Brookfield, CT: Millbrook Press.

Yorinks, A. (1986). *Hey, Al!* New York: Farrar, Straus and Giroux.

Ziefert, H. (2003). *Zoo Parade!* Maplewood, NJ: Blue Apple Books.

Appendix A

A1.   APPLE

A4.   RABBIT EAR

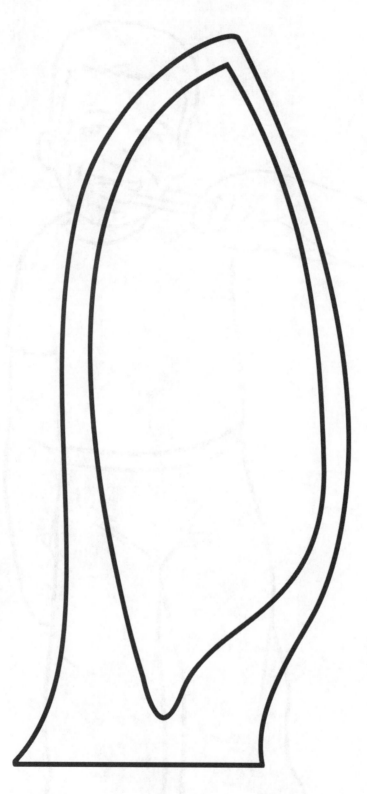

A5. BEE

A6. FLOWER

A7. EGG

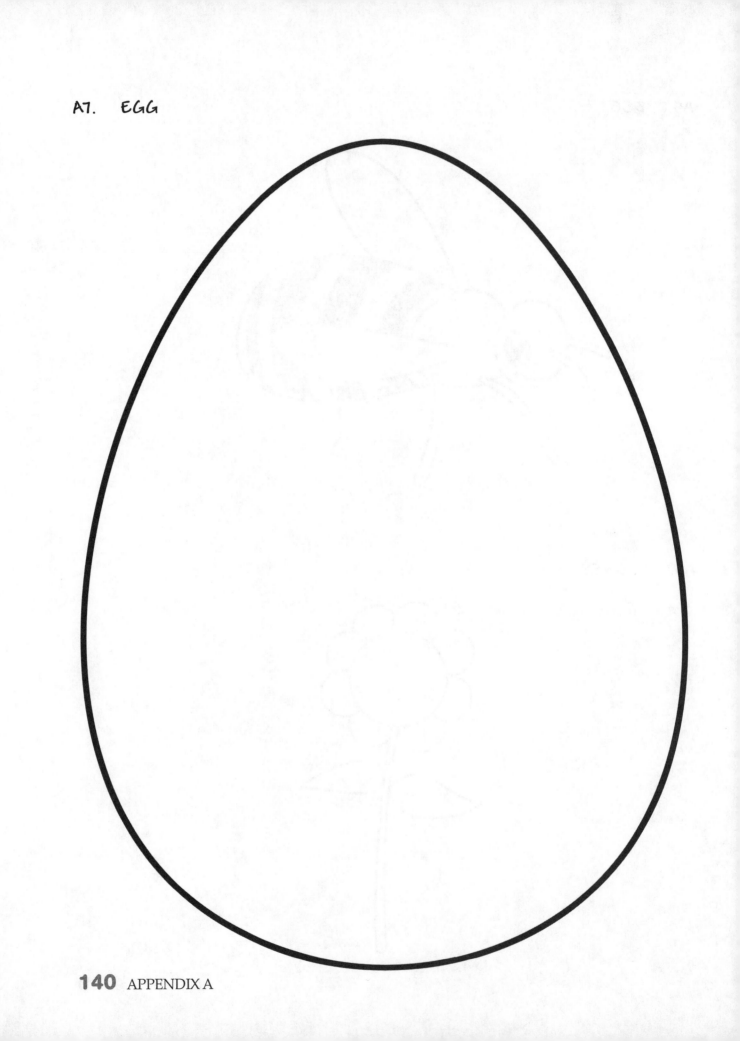

A8. DOCTOR

A9. DENTIST

A10. POLICE OFFICER

A12. MAIL CARRIER

A14. DINOSAUR BINGO CARDS

A15. FISH

A16. FROG

A17. WATERING CAN

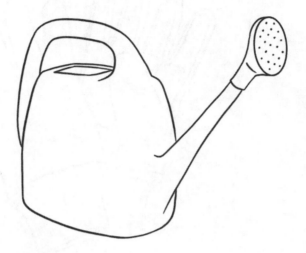

A18. SHOVEL

A19. GARDEN GLOVES

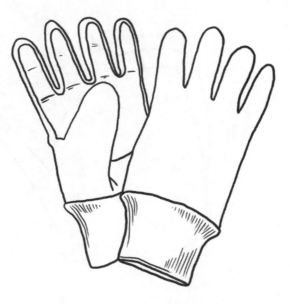

A20. SPADE

A21. SEEDS

A22. SMALL FLOWER

A23. LILY PAD

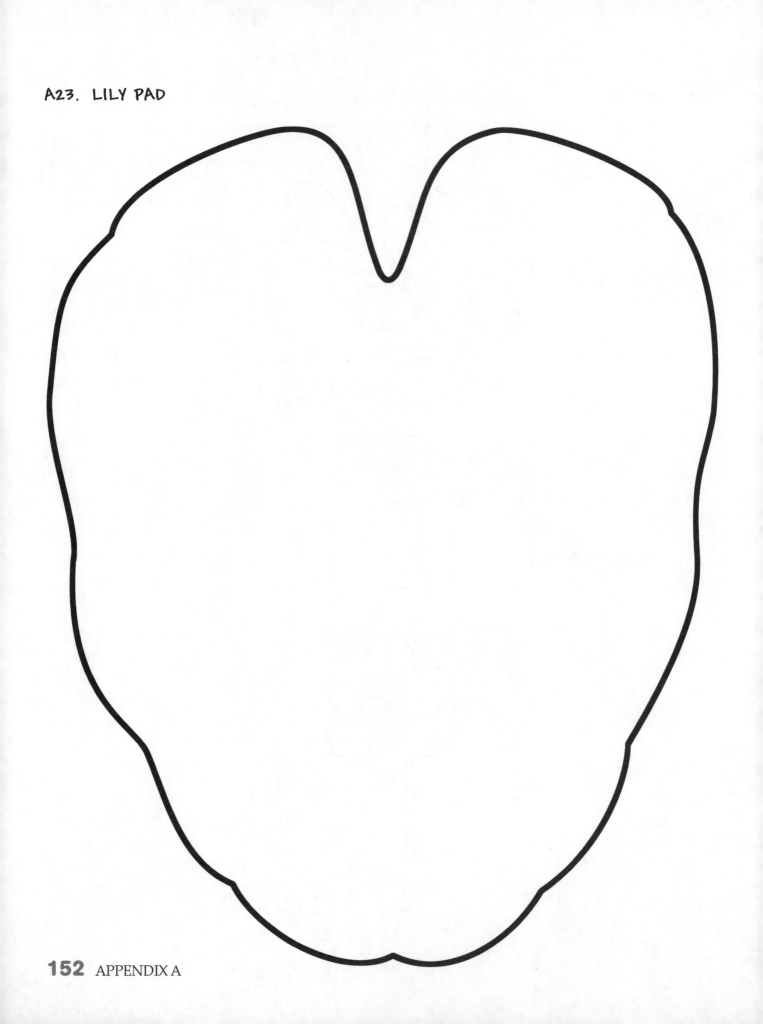

A24. COW

A26. TREE

A27. TULIP

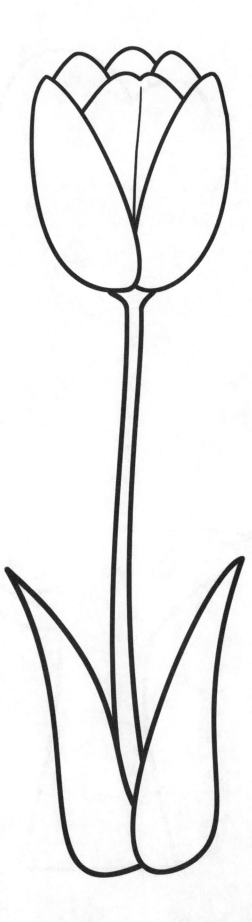

A28. TOUCAN

A29. HORSE HEAD

Appendix B

LETTER 1

Dear Family:

We will be talking about families next week. Please send in a picture of your child and his or her family members. These may be sent as separate photos or as a group picture. Please send the picture(s) in by [date needed].

Thank you for your help!

Sincerely,

LETTER 2

Dear Family:

We will be talking about pets next week. Please send in a photo or photos of your pets by [date photos are needed]. If you do not have any pets, please let your child cut out a picture of a pet that he or she would like, from a magazine or newspaper, or you may print a picture of a pet found on the Internet or on a computer disc.

Thank you for your help!

Sincerely,

LETTER 3

Dear Family:

We are going to have a teddy bears' picnic on [date of picnic]. Please have your child bring his or her teddy bear or favorite stuffed animal on that day. Also, please write your child's name on his or her toy. You may either write on the animal's tag or label the toy by writing your child's name on a piece of masking tape.

Thank you for your help!

Sincerely,

Index of Units

Index